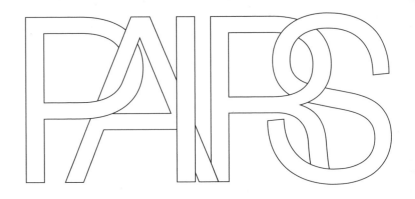

Edited by Nicolás Delgado Álcega, Vladimir Gintoff,
Kimberley Huggins, and Kyle Winston

Distributed by Harvard University Press
London, England and Cambridge, Massachusetts

EDITORS	Nicolás Delgado Álcega
	Vladimir Gintoff
	Kimberley Huggins
	Kyle Winston
CONTRIBUTORS	Emma Lewis
	Elisa Ngan
	Maxwell Smith-Holmes
GRAPHIC DESIGN	Normal:
	Renata Graw and Lucas Reif
COVER	Aryn Beitz
PRINTING	Grafiche Veneziane
	Società Cooperative
COPYEDITING	Arts Editing Services:
	Tyler Considine and Liz Janoff
ADVISORS	Kyle K. Courtney, Ken Stewart,
	Marielle Suba, Sarah M. Whiting,
	and Inés Zalduendo

THANKS — *Pairs* Issue 02 would not have been possible without the generosityand support of Marc Angélil, Rossana Hu, Serein Liu, Junxi Lu, Christine O'Brien, Alix Reiskind, and Helen Zhang.

PAIRS — *Pairs* was founded in 2019 by Nicolás Delgado Álcega, Vladimir Gintoff, and Kimberley Huggins, with the support of Dean Sarah M. Whiting and the Harvard University Graduate School of Design.

Letter from the Editors

When we launched our first issue, Giovanna Borasi, the director of the Canadian Centre for Architecture, said *Pairs* had a certain *prima voltita*, Italian for "first timeness," the charm of fresh and fearless enthusiasm behind an early endeavor. And while surely imperfect, our first issue was a genuine effort with clear character and direction. Considering this, the second issue offered an exciting opportunity both to refine the journal's purpose and to establish a trajectory. While still unable to experiment with the in-person archive digging that we originally conceived, and limited to working remotely, we focused inward and wondered: Where do we go from here?

This issue has reinforced that editing is a slow and persistent process. We've learned that meaning is not simply found in the conversations with our guests but rather something unearthed over time. Each contribution to *Pairs* begins with the hope for an insightful and surprising dialogue with someone we admire. When we find ourselves rereading transcripts at the start of the editing process, we are often surprised by the erasure of certain qualities of a verbal exchange and the emergence of details spoken but not initially heard. As we discover new and layered interpretations while editing, the depth of the exchange shows itself to us. Many of the most remarkable ideas revealed themselves only after repeatedly revisiting a conversation—an experience we hope readers will share.

These conclusions may come as no surprise to designers. In Issue 01, Piet Oudolf described his practice—his firsthand work in the garden and photographs taken for reference—as a form of editing. This reminded us that this process could be as essential to design as it is to writing. Piet compared editing to bringing the parts of a garden into proportion over time, to balancing the demands of a plant that may grow more quickly with those of another that may only show itself years after planting. For us, as students of design, it was a recognition that powerful and unanticipated outcomes often emerge from long periods of iteration. It encouraged us to release the immense pressure placed on the intentions behind design work and embrace a method of give-and-take. In this reflective mode, creativity is not removed from important realities, it exists within a balance of the intentions behind our work and the effects of design practice.

While finishing Issue 02, we read *A Swim in a Pond in the Rain*, in which George Saunders describes the relationship between writer and reader—the literary pair—as two figures dropping pebbles into either end of a pond, where their ripples eventually reach one another and form a relationship. "These days," Saunders writes, "it's easy to feel that we've fallen out of connection with one another and with the earth and with reason and with love. I mean: we have. But to read, to write, is to say that we still believe in, at least, the *possibility* of connection." Saunders's words resonated with us: *This is the point of Pairs!*

In bringing subjects and objects to a common table, we invite them to make something new together and share that result. But putting something out in the world for interaction and critique requires that we make ourselves vulnerable to others. We acknowledge that we can never represent each subject or object in its full complexity. The pair comes with its own constraints, just like any design problem. However, through confronting imperfect opportunities and being unsure about what the right course of action may be, we have found the most rewarding work. This is our way of bringing things into proportion, of taking a chance on what we think is right and passing it on to you.

Nicolás, Vladimir, Kimberley, and Kyle

Paola Sturla

with Elisa Ngan

Philips Pavilion

On Data and Intuition

ELISA NGAN   Le Corbusier's name is stamped on the Philips Pavilion, but in our correspondence you mentioned that you studied Iannis Xenakis's contributions to it. Why not Le Corbusier's?

PAOLA STURLA   You imagine someone like Le Corbusier as the protagonist all the time, but, in fact, he was not. He designed the *Poème Électronique*, the show for the interior, but the shape of the building was the work of Iannis Xenakis. The relationship between them, how Le Corbusier set the requirements for the process, how Xenakis defined the form through mathematics, the requirement to showcase Philips products as much as possible, the constraint of architecture to build a self-carrying base, and the use of concrete despite the temporality of the building—to me, this was very, very intriguing. The fact that Le Corbusier surrounded himself with such high-profile professionals to come out with this form somehow suggested to me that while this building is inspired by technology and is made possible by technology, it's still a product of minds and people collaborating, people being influenced by their environment.

George Kubler wrote an interesting book, *The Shape of Time*, on how certain artifacts become part of history because they end the complex set of lines that is history itself by resonating with culture in a specific moment. Le Corbusier created this kind of artifact by surrounding himself with young high-profile professionals who contributed to deliver the pavilion. It's the effort of teamwork.

EN   He needed to figure out how to communicate that complexity as well. There are so many different diagrams and blueprints for this project.

PS   The score that Le Corbusier set to try to bring everything together—the rounded one, the circle one, yeah, this one—it reminds me a lot of the work of Lawrence Halprin, the landscape architect. Halprin came to a very simple representation of the design process and his own work, which asks, "What is

11

Louis Kalff (client), Le Corbusier (architect), and Edgard Varèse (composer) conversing in front of the Philips Pavilion.

the experience of a landscape?" This particular representation is trying to convey something similar: What's the experience of the Pavilion? What's the experience of the *Poème Électronique*?

People get into that stomach-shaped building and go through a very narrow threshold. Then, they get into the more vertical space with projections on the walls, and there is this very primitive Dolby system that surrounds them in a collective experience. And finally, they get out on the other side. That's a kind of aesthetic experience of a space. The representations tell me that Le Corbusier approached the program with a landscape-oriented mentality.

If you consider a landscape as the experience of a place from the inside, you experience it from a subjective and emotional point of view rather than as a top-down abstract visualization. I would say that Le Corbusier is narrating an impression of the pavilion and choreographing an interior experience, similar to Lawrence Halprin.

PAOLA STURLA WITH ELISA NGAN

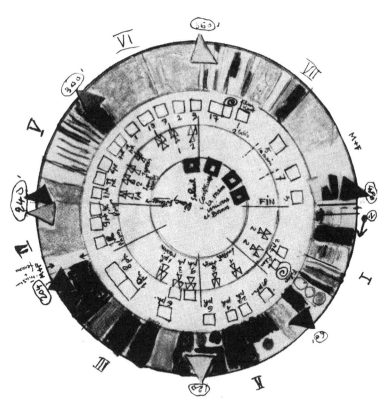

Early version of the minutage organizing the looped sequence of colors and sound in a circular diagrammatic form.

EN   Choreography was hard as well. At one point, the project developed over three different continents. It may have been the first time a team was so distributed. Today, remote collaboration and technical support for collaborative work is second nature for the design industry. What do you think designers today can learn from this pavilion when we consider collaboration as part of our practice?

PS   It's going to be more and more interesting in the future to go back to examples like the one in the Philips Pavilion to see how even with technology around—because this is a heavily technological building for the time it was designed and built—the leadership of the process is somehow still in the hands of the designer. The designer, in order to control or even tackle such a complexity, has to surround himself with experts and other people who do different things. What we do at the end is not just manufacture objects but deliver them through a process that functions on contemporary culture.

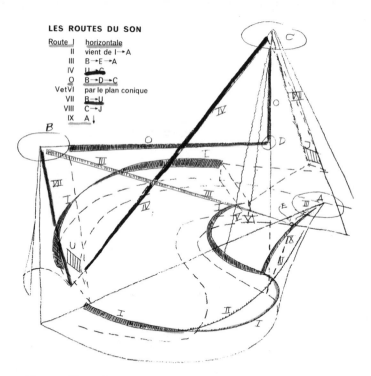

LES ROUTES DU SON

Route I   horizontale
    II   vient de I→A
    III   B→E→A
    IV   U→C
    O   B→D→C
VetVI   par le plan conique
    VII   B→U
    VIII   C→J
    IX   A↓

Diagram of "sound routes" for Varèse's composition to travel in relation to the geometry of Xenakis's pavilion.

EN To handle that complexity, do we need to be tied to the typical medium of a field? Do you think that students at the GSD need to design buildings if they're architects or landscapes if they're landscape architects or urban plans if they're urban planners to better control this process? Where is the designer located?

PS That's another interesting question. It's something I care a lot about. I think it's more interesting to reflect on the design process itself. What do we do? Pulling from Umberto Eco and Lidia Gasperoni, I call it the "humanistic approach." A humanist is someone who needs to tackle complex issues and not mere problems, someone who digs into and goes across different fields in the constant flow of knowledge to try to interpret and affect through the shape of what they do the context of these new objects. The designer is the last humanist.

When professors give students a brief, we tend not to over clarify every point of the brief. There are open questions: How will you improve this situation? What will you do there? How will you design a service/building/landscape that will improve something? Or change something? Or make something possible for a client?

The team tuning the music to the space for optimal acoustics.

To find that answer is an iterative process. It reshapes the shape, and by "shape," I mean something very broad. A shape could be the structure of an application, or it could be the form of a landform in a landscape. It could be a wide variety of things. But the important thing is that it's *poietic*: the preferred way of design goes beyond the analysis. *Poietic* means that it's related to making. The designer *makes* something. The knowledge gets expressed through something new that appears at the end of this process or during this process. We *make* things, wherever, whatever they are.

EN   What about the challenges in parsing through what the vision actually is? The romantic notion of collaboration is often, at the end of the day, an assembly of experts with their own opinions and disciplinary baggage. Making things can become managing stakeholders—and not in the creative sense as exercised by Le Corbusier. How do you see designers operating within those types of challenges?

PS   When I started working in engineering, I definitely hit my nose on that. The people I worked with were all male super experts with 30-plus years of experience in doing exactly that thing. I found that my drawings and my designs were actually negotiation tools. I was using the form of what I was doing, which at that time was landscapes, as material to start conversations with them, so at least we had something to discuss. You have to remember that all the other professionals are designers as well. They apply the same iterative methodology.

EN   It is the same … but isn't it also different? When it comes to methods, we now have this data-driven "objective" kind of knowledge versus something that's more humanistic and interpretive. "Intuition" has become almost a dirty word, pregnant with potential bias. Leaning into the interpretive has become more fraught.

PS   We all know, as designers, that there is a lot of interpretation in what we do. It's not an objective profession. It draws on our biases and our tastes, our life experiences and design experiences. It seems obvious to have to remark that what we do is not objective, but it's because of the contemporary rise of a specific set of digital technologies, which pretend to deliver objective analyses, that we think it's possible to come out with the receipt for the perfect design.

      The data-driven and the humanistic are parts of the same process. I would say the designer is always the director of that process. The designer is always asking, "Why are we doing that? What are we doing? What for? What's the endgame of what we are doing?"

EN   Jill Lepore, an American history professor at Harvard, had a recent talk about the growth of data science programs. She was feeling frustrated about the lack of epistemic understanding of what a data science program would even look like or who a data scientist even is. Her point was that, at the end of the day, we all work and have been working with data, even if it is not explicitly positioned that way. It's interesting to take on that new role of data scientist, unpack its popular development within a technology context, and then imagine how design fits in, especially when the designer, an interpretative role much like the historian, is so much older in comparison. Does the designer have to be worried about their role being subjugated and disappearing? Do they need to be territorial?

PS   Yes, I think so. I think that the designer has to care about that a lot. I think that the topic you're bringing up about the epistemology of data analysis is super important. If you're talking to a professional statistician, they know all of this. They know the limits of statistics, and they know that statistics are, at the end, interpretation. Because to some extent, they are designers too. They design their own studies; they design their own parameters; they design the criteria. Even if you are working with an unsupervised machine-learning algorithm, you're still writing the algorithm. There is still human agency involved.

In that chain of responsibility there is an interesting debate and an interesting topic to tackle. As designers, we're familiar with the idea of delivering something that can imply the responsibility of having to make a choice or a chain of choices. Being confident about being the ones that *can* make the choice will empower us to face the world and inspire people to have a completely different attitude: the attitude of a leader rather than the attitude of a follower. I really hope it will be a greater and greater part of the design curricula.

EN   It's a very political act to say that these are the choices we should make. Some of us don't trust ourselves. It's easier to be a technocrat and let something else make the hard decisions.

PS   What I've seen in my experience is that students tend to rely a lot on data. When we suddenly ask them to come up with a design and express it in the visual language of drawings, they may feel lost and try to prove what they are doing *through data*. I can totally sympathize with students who try to find help in functionalist parametric software and data, who say, "Oh, the data told me that. The computer did that. The simulation is telling me that." And I'll respond, "What are the parameters of the simulation?"

Data analysis is a design operation in itself. It's not delivering objective results. A design student might not be the best data scientist but will be the best at making something out of that result, interpreting that result into a form of some sort. It's very important for students to understand that whenever they use data, it's still their decision. It's still their point. They're making a point.

EN   If they're deciding the parameters and interpreting what those parameters should be, then what you're describing doesn't sound too different from the process that Le Corbusier and his team went through.

17

34

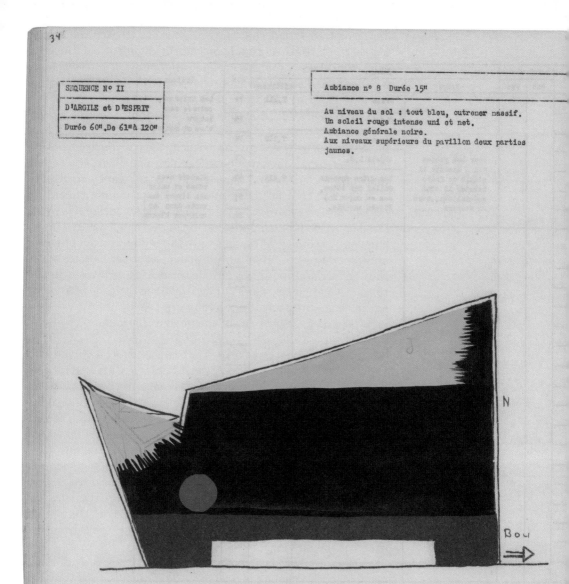

SÉQUENCE N° II

D'ARGILE et D'ESPRIT

Durée 60". De 61" à 120"

Ambiance n° 8 Durée 15"

Au niveau du sol : tout bleu, outremer massif.
Un soleil rouge intense uni et net.
Ambiance générale noire.
Aux niveaux supérieurs du pavillon deux parties
jaunes.

Sec	Volumes		Ecrans			Sec	Tritons	Paroles
	Mat	Fom	Notes	Vision	Référence			
81				Les quatre savants	T.113	81	Les quatre savants dans les trous éclairés en couleur bleu et rouge.	
82						82		
83				↓		83		
84			Toutes ces têtes seront animées,	Tête de nègre Congo	T.114	84		
85			c'est-à-dire qu'il faut à tout	Tête de nègre Maori	T.116	85		
86			prix éviter la monotonie et la	Tête de nègre Mayogo	T.117	86		
87			lenteur. Cela doit être	Tête de fille Mongbetu	T.118	87		
88			vivant	Courbet femme couchée FAH 227	D.121	88	Les tritons en couleur bleu et rouge.	
89				Art Attique MAL 49	D.124	89		
90				Art Sumérien MAL 11	D.125	90		
91				Egypte MAL 68	D.128	91		
92				Dame D'Echo MAZ 94	D.130	92		
93				Art Sumérien MAL 11	D.125	93	↓	
94				César MAL 171	D.133	94		
95				Art Celtique MAL 212	D.135	95		

Excerpts from the minutage choreographing color, music, and images. Each sequence shows an evolution from a radial to a sectional organizational schema and tables with a key of five primary colors.

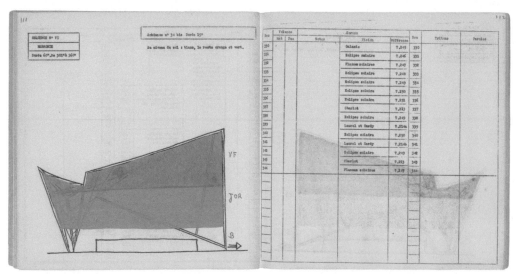

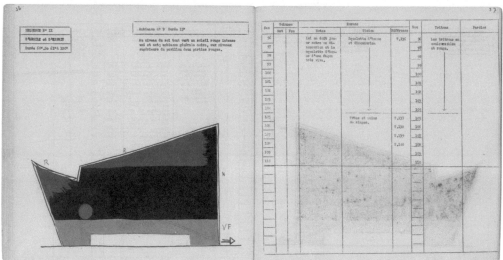

PAOLA STURLA WITH ELISA NGAN

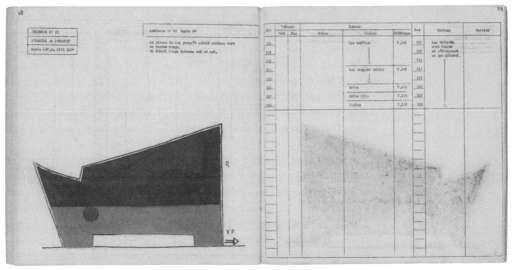

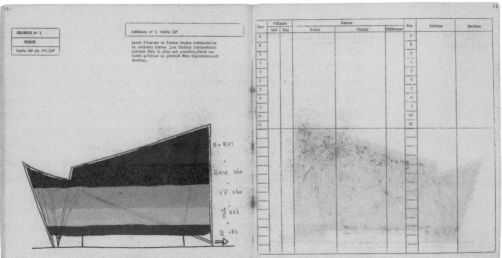

Excerpts from the minutage choreographing color, music, and images. Each
sequence shows an evolution from a radial to a sectional organizational schema
and tables with a key of five primary colors.

PS　　The idea is there is no linear process of collaborative inter-disciplinary work, as in the case of the pavilion and in the case of every practitioner who wants to deliver something in the physical world these days. It's the part of the work that will be so hard to automate in the future, and that, in my opinion, is what students should learn in design school today. For a practitioner, it's obvious. But it's that kind of obvious that is very hard to put into words, and that's why, in my opinion, it's hardly recorded in the academic stream of knowledge.

　　　　Imagine you are learning, literally, how to make a physical model. How would you describe that process? There are elements that are intuitive, that are practice-based. You just learn how to do it without knowing how to explain it. Donald Schön called it the "reflection-in-action" process. To explain that, he used the example of a desk crit in architecture school, how you deliver that knowledge to the students by going through a process of trial and error in the studio.

EN　　I'm glad you brought up the architecture studio because, as a vehicle to learn how to design, it's a super interesting mechanism. One of the reasons why I personally found the GSD's Master in Design Engineering program so compelling is that it is set up as a collaborative studio. Having gone through actual architecture studios, this is almost an oxymoron to me, so of course I wanted to experience the experimental drama.

　　　　Now that I've been through the MDE studios, I feel like its promise of collaboration anchors it in a locus of Silicon Valley design thinking, where the focal point of design has shifted toward the user and "finding" their needs by executing upon a set of tasks that will magically produce or uncover an objective answer, similar to what you were saying about data-driven design. Compare this to the studio, a Beaux-Arts tradition that has always been less about collaboration and more about intensely investigating and iterating on the design outcome in a master–apprentice way that can be very personal, interpretive, and, as you say, reflective. It's just my opinion, but this is a methodological tension that I don't think is fully resolved within the program. I would argue that the studio, the space, is the real commitment though, not the processual methods, which should be continually invented and refreshed anyway to fit with the evolution of the problem space. Where else can you experience the commitment necessary to learn how to design?

PS　　Right, and there is no way you can learn how to design in a theory class. It doesn't work like that. It's a matter of learning by doing. The GSD has a long legacy of this. That's why,

22

to some extent, data can feed your creative process, but at some point, you have to translate that into form. To translate that into form, you don't follow any logical rule. It's a process influenced by a variety of contingencies.

After all, design is related to context, and by "context," I don't mean only the place, building, landscape, garden, or whatever product we seek but really the cultural context.

EN How do you decide what cultural context needs to be brought in and included in the choreography? That's a choice that all the data in the world can't make for you.

PS Exactly. Where do you cut the information? That's the real design decision: you're deciding what data to feed into the process. That's the first critical decision. Then, you're getting an output, and you still have to pick from the options what would make sense for the working context. That's the next critical design decision.

Sure, the algorithm might suggest I use a certain shape, but will that shape be innovative? I don't know. Even if you use another neural network and somehow just settle on doing the opposite, it's still the opposite of something that already exists.

There is no out-of-scope contribution, like the musician with the architect, as Corbusier called upon Varèse. Is the algorithm trained to suggest, "Hey, by the way, yes, these 1,000 plazas are amazing, but what if you call a musician?"

I am not against these tools in principle, but let's keep in mind that they don't deliver objectivity.

David Hartt &
Sharon Johnston

with Vladimir Gintoff

Stirling's Sketches of Sackler

On New Museums and Distributing Culture

VLADIMIR GINTOFF   David, you're an artist who works with architectural concepts. Sharon, you're an architect who has collaborated extensively with artists. Could you talk about how art and architecture intersect in your practices and how you came to collaborate?

SHARON JOHNSTON   I'll start with something easy, which is how we met. Johnston Marklee was selected to design a master plan and a phase-one renovation of the Museum of Contemporary Art Chicago. Madeleine Grynsztejn runs an especially dynamic board for the museum, and David was a member.

Not too long after we got started, Mark [Lee] and I had to think about how a number of different spaces might function for the museum and what they might be called. David, you emailed us, quietly nudging us to begin conceptualizing a particular space, the winter garden, and about how spaces like it function not only in museums or in Chicago but in civic spaces around the world. This started our conversation about precedents. This was important as we were getting to know the museum board, and everyone had their own initiatives they needed to get across. David, you cut right through that. Those early dialogues are emblematic of why artists are so important to our office: because of the conceptual clarity in how artists think about the world.

We've invited David into other projects as a thought partner, and he continues to provide profound insights. His sense of space and perception of atmosphere is really acute, and we've drawn from it as friends and collaborators ever since.

DAVID HARTT   Thank you for that. I think that our relationship and desire to continue working together in different contexts has flourished because we share a desire to participate. It's very easy to sit on the outside and critique. It's more difficult to actually engage and offer ideas about solving problems. I

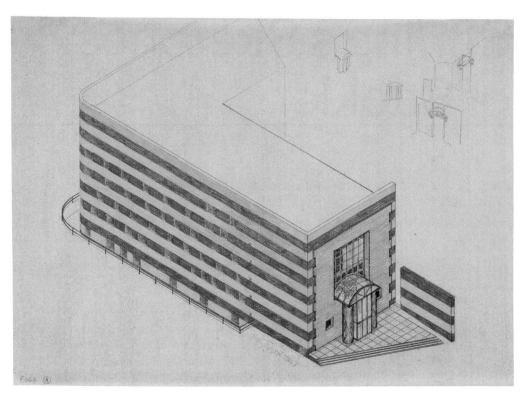

Drawing for the Arthur M. Sackler Museum, Axonometric Color Study for Broadway and Quincy Street Elevations, 1982.140.7.

DAVID HARTT & SHARON JOHNSTON WITH VLADIMIR GINTOFF

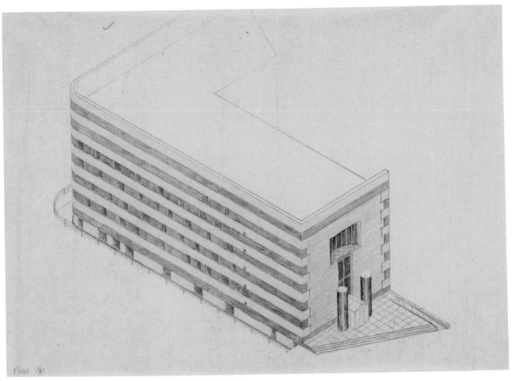

Drawing for the Arthur M. Sackler Museum, Axonometric Color Study for
Broadway and Quincy Street Elevations, 1982.140.8.

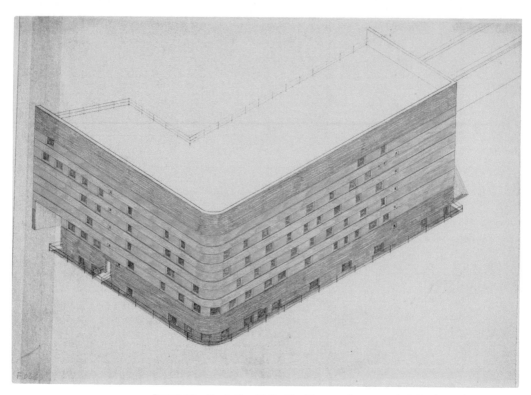

Drawing for the Arthur M. Sackler Museum, Axonometric Color Study for Cambridge and Quincy Street Elevations, 1982.140.11.

DAVID HARTT & SHARON JOHNSTON WITH VLADIMIR GINTOFF

VG   David, you've said that your work uses architecture as a proxy to unpack ideas surrounding race, place, economics, and politics. In some ways, this sounds like the brief for an architecture project. I'm curious if you've ever considered engaging in architecture in a more collaborative capacity or even teaching in an architecture-studio setting?

really cherish that aspect of our dialogues because it gives me an opportunity to think alongside you about ideas that I care about, big problems about which artists don't usually get a say. To be able to participate meaningfully is such a great privilege.

VG   David, you've said that your work uses architecture as a proxy to unpack ideas surrounding race, place, economics, and politics. In some ways, this sounds like the brief for an architecture project. I'm curious if you've ever considered engaging in architecture in a more collaborative capacity or even teaching in an architecture-studio setting?

DH   That's a great question. I find myself increasingly drawn into the field of architecture, but I also think that one of the really important things about being an artist is the capacity to occupy different kinds of positions. I can borrow from the methodologies of architecture or anthropology or law or any of these different disciplines but not necessarily worry about being governed by orthodoxies that restrict my ability to approach problems or solve problems using different means.

I did a project a few years ago that was a commission from Illinois Institute of Technology for the Mies van der Rohe Crown Hall Prize where I photographed seven finalists' projects. I wasn't interested in just documenting the buildings—these were all incredibly famous buildings that had been photographed countless times. What I was more interested in doing was trying to understand them from the perspective of people who use them every day. So, I was really trying to understand the dimensions of use, habitation, and belonging. For me, an aspect of architecture that's super important but rarely dealt with is the lives of a building. A lot of the work I've been doing lately stems from that, from trying to understand the lives of buildings, the lives of spaces.

SJ   Some things we strive for in our work are not heroic moments but nuanced and generous spaces, an architecture that accommodates different inhabitations. That's what drives us to make institutional buildings that are not monumental but more enmeshed in the context that they exist in. At least that's the hope. Ideas of the ephemeral, the oblique, and these fleeting, cinematic moments in architecture are where David, Mark, and I really intersect. These qualities often have the greatest effect on the way we remember spaces and how we really experience buildings.

29

VG   Thinking about that, Sharon, you and Mark have a history of working on designs for art spaces, such as the Chile House and the Pavilion of Six Views, both from around a decade ago, and more recent large-scale projects such as the Menil Drawing Institute and the forthcoming Philadelphia Contemporary. How has your understanding of art institutions changed as you've created them?

SJ   After practicing for 20 years, it's interesting to think about the kinds of people and organizations that become part of your orbit. We've been really fortunate that the institutions and foundations we've worked with are truly searching for something. In the case of Harry Philbrick at Philadelphia Contemporary, he's been in the world of museums for his whole career but really has a vision of something new. Harry wants this project to be about a journey, an institution that reflects his understanding of a world that's changing really fast.

What people expect from a museum experience is continually evolving. The expectation is, of course, to see art, but the museum is becoming a more complex place where exhibitions are just part of the experience. You can go there and have meetings or have a meal. I think the aspiration for a lot of institutions that we work with is to make the art experience about an engagement with artists and ideas, and we are trying to expand this possibility in contemporary art spaces.

VG   On the subject of spaces and their evolutions, I've asked that we discuss a set of James Stirling's sketches for the Arthur M. Sackler Building on Harvard's campus. When it opened in 1985, it was partly a museum, but now it's only an educational space. The controversy surrounding the Sackler family and their philanthropy, which was enabled by their pharmaceutical business, is well-established, though the building's name has not been changed.

It's obvious that institutions need to show accountability for the gifts and endowments that fund their agendas. What does the Sackler case tell us about how museums and other philanthropically supported entities should function going forward?

DH   There are so many issues here that I think it's really important to thread the needle carefully. It's important to have a nuanced understanding of where we sit individually and it's also important to have a stance and to register our politics. I want to make sure of that because we are touching on things that people feel strongly about. What I want is for those possibilities, those positions and politics to stand independently from our roles. One doesn't erase the other but rather they stand in counterpoint.

In my experience as a trustee on the boards of two institutions, if the art world really wants to hold people accountable, those boards would thin out really quickly. You don't get that rich without fucking over at least someone, right? I think there's a huge difference between exploitation in business just as part of doing business and the kind of criminal behavior of the Sackler family, in terms of their responsibility for the crisis caused by the drug that they produced and marketed knowing that it caused massive harm to people's health.

SJ   This may be too idealistic, but if we look to museums as places of debate and exchange, could there be a kind of productive reckoning? A course of action for both artists and people who support museums financially that could lead to something better? Is there a way that diverse agendas could coexist more productively?

Linking this specifically to the Sackler Building: it's a fascinating piece of architecture with a unique lineage to talk about these issues. First, there's a kind of inherent incompleteness to the building because it was intended to connect to the Fogg Museum across the street, but that never happened. It's also a teaching museum, so it's a hybrid building. It has both classrooms and galleries. It also has a kind of peculiar context, engaging both seminal institutional buildings on the Harvard campus on Quincy Street and the more prosaic neighborhood buildings. It's full of contradictions.

I'm also intrigued by the fact that the Fogg became the "Harvard Art Museums," which subsumed all of the satellite institutions within the new Renzo Piano building. With that change, the Sackler Building became the History of Art and Architecture building. This emphasizes the point that architecture rarely serves one function permanently. Buildings are designed to be transformed. It's interesting to think about patronage through that evolution, to think about how the imprint it leaves on a building can evolve.

DH   I love that you mentioned that it is a teaching institution and the role that different artifacts play. I teach at Penn, and the Penn Museum has an encyclopedic collection: Egyptian sphinxes, pre-Columbian artifacts, objects from different Indigenous tribes throughout the Americas. It's just chock full of 150 years of examples of colonial exploitation. But these objects also serve a vital role on the campus, in terms of providing examples for the departments of anthropology,

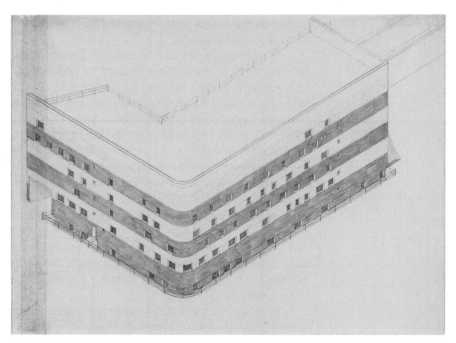

Drawing for the Arthur M. Sackler Museum, Axonometric Color Study for Cambridge and Quincy Street Elevations, 1982.140.12.

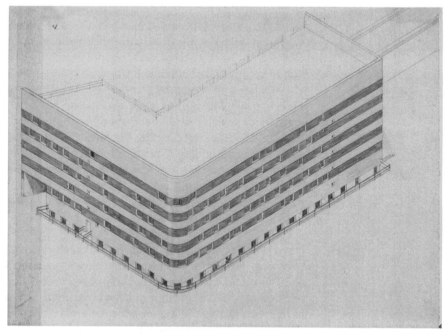

Drawing for the Arthur M. Sackler Museum, Axonometric Color Study for Cambridge and Quincy Street Elevations, 1982.140.10.

DAVID HARTT & SHARON JOHNSTON WITH VLADIMIR GINTOFF

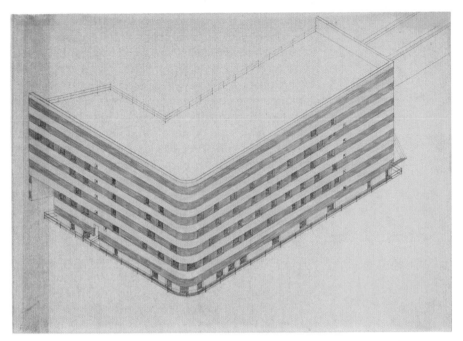

Drawing for the Arthur M. Sackler Museum, Axonometric Color Study for Cambridge and Quincy Street Elevations, 1982.140.14.

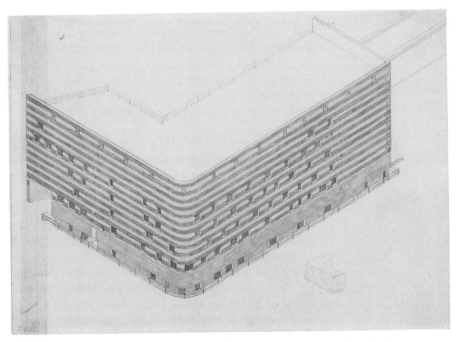

Drawing for the Arthur M. Sackler Museum, Axonometric Color Study for Cambridge and Quincy Street Elevations, 1982.140.13.

archaeology, and sociology. They need access to these materials. They need to understand them. The objects bring a whole wealth of material evidence to how we see and understand cultures.

What I think is important is that these questions are being asked right now. It's important that these issues are no longer beyond reproach and that we are thinking through ideas of accountability, of who has the right to speak for certain histories or care for objects and artifacts that are products of specific cultures. How do we house them? How do we ensure that people have access to them? How do we preserve them and steward them for the future? How do we contextualize them properly?

I think it's beautifully ironic that the Stirling design is postmodern, which in many ways indicates a kind of deracination of all these historical reference points. The architectural elements become free-floating signifiers that no longer necessarily speak to specific cultural histories but instead serve as almost pure style. So, the building itself is kind of negotiating its own disconnection from some of these ideas and responsibilities. Perhaps the Fogg initiative grounds it and forces it to consider these things again.

VG   Sticking with philanthropy, Sharon, the Menil Collection is a private museum funded through an endowment created by John and Dominique de Menil. This setup allows for free admission and distinguishes the Menil from other institutions that rely on ticket sales to cover operating costs. Considering this, how do you think architecture can respond to a different set of priorities for institutions, ones that might be more equitable and less driven by the bottom line?

SJ   I think most cultural institutions today are wrestling with these issues. Of course, it starts with a question "Does it cost money to get through the door?" But I also think organizations are thinking deeply even about where to situate themselves in the city. It's becoming a more pivotal question about how to build relationships. Philadelphia Contemporary's foundational principle is about partnership. Rather than acting as a sole institution going it alone, it's founded on the principles of collaboration and sharing and creating platforms for exchange.

As institutions try to get closer to their audiences, they're going to be questioning their environments and how much architecture is needed to be an institution. The boundaries between institutions and their audiences and their cities and contexts are becoming provocatively more and more porous.

That's really exciting for Mark and me, but I don't think every architect will be thrilled because a lot of the time the shifts taking place aren't about architecture. The solution isn't architecture. It's allowing artists and audiences to engage in more tangible ways beyond the white cube.

What's so special about the Menil is that it's not just about a couple of buildings but rather all the space around them too. Reyner Banham has talked about how the Menil campus is a neighborhood for art. And it truly is that. It's the park, the porch, the bungalows, the museum. It's all of that together, that mise-en-scène of things that make it approachable. For us, in order to be challenged by and excited about ideas that artists put forward, there needs to be a level of comfort to feel engaged with those concepts.

DH   Yeah, that's so brilliantly said. I also think it's important to recognize that you don't have to run a museum as a business. That in itself is a neoliberal myth, right? The idea that a museum somehow needs to pay for itself in order for it to be sustainable is, I think, an absolute misconception. The same distinction could apply to a lot of different institutions that we value that make up critical parts of our society and culture.

One thing I understand as a professor—and I think you've probably experienced the same thing, Sharon—is that at times it can feel transactional, right? You can feel like, "I'm paid to be here, and you're paying to come here, and we're going to exchange these ideas and things." There's a kind of artifice, in terms of what's holding the experience together. Especially as artists, there are so many intangibles that govern why we participate. If you want to get rich, there are far better ways to be in the world and professions that you could explore. Instead, it's about ideas of community and contributing to a culture that we find valuable.

Moving from a transactional model to one where both sides feel equally committed to the establishment of a culture that we both have to contribute to, even if it comes at a loss to our own wealth or well-being, contributes to the health of that culture and needs to be reciprocated by all participants. As soon as someone comes in and treats an educational institution as a transactional environment, it compromises the integrity of what allows those environments to grow and thrive. I think we need to think about museums in those terms. We need to stop putting the emphasis on the cost of admission or the value of the works inside and focus more holistically on the role that museums play within their city or region.

DAVID HARTT & SHARON JOHNSTON WITH VLADIMIR GINTOFF

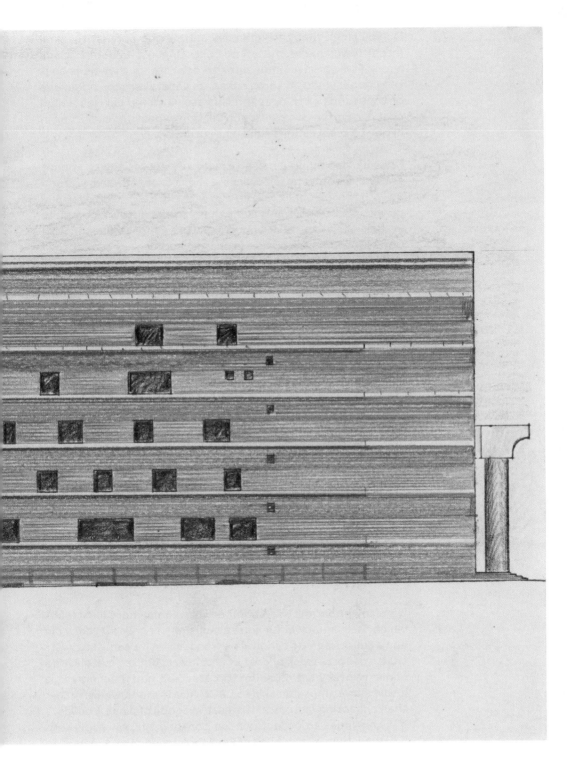

STIRLING'S SKETCHES OF SACKLER

VG   Do you think that through a reconfiguration of institutional intent fewer museums will be collecting institutions? I think a lot of what drives museums to operate as they do is that they're assigned, in some cases, as caretakers for hundreds of thousands of things, and this stewardship carries a high cost. Do we have to give up on certain aspects of collecting in order to create more agile institutions?

DH   Stewardship fulfills a massive role in museums and an important one. If someone isn't playing the role of steward, you end up with the Acropolis, you end up with the Colosseum, you end up with these enormous ruins that are absolutely incomplete in their ability to reflect upon a culture's most valued institutions. Museums are critical in preserving our very sense of self.

SJ   It's a question of building a whole ecosystem. In Philadelphia, there's the Philadelphia Museum of Art, there's Philadelphia Contemporary, and then there are all the things in between. That's the only viable way forward anyway because institutions like the PMA are not going to emerge out of nothing anymore. There's too much history for them to ever amass that kind of material. But I think younger institutions are not necessarily acting in a parasitical way. They're considering questions like, "How do we create environments that can house great historic works, maintain a level of stewardship that requires expensive HVAC and humidity control, and combine that with a harbor space for graffiti artists to teach kids about color?"

       I think that moving forward—whether it's inside an institution or a hybrid institution that produces shows in the city and has a hub somewhere else—these kinds of models that bring different worlds into contact are really exciting and attractive. There are still wealthy patrons who want to build museums for themselves and their collections, but for other newer institutions, it's the messier, more interesting hybrid models that are driving the way people are thinking.

VG   It's also important to remember that somewhere like MoMA, which feels so powerful and established, is only 90 years old and a collecting institution. The "modern" in its name suggests that it collects work of only a certain era, but ultimately it's a contemporary art museum too. Maybe it could become this grand survey museum akin to LACMA or the Met, where rather than collecting historical things, the scope of what it collects, if it continues to collect contemporaneously, will represent a comprehensive account of work produced over a long span of time.

38

I wonder if an institution like MoMA needs to establish a cutoff for itself where it says, "We're going to yield contemporary art to other, younger institutions and focus on a particular era and scope in what we've collected and what we want to represent."

DH   There's also what the Fogg achieved in having to change and adapt, right? So, even thinking about an institution as being fixed and defined by its geography and the envelope of the building is, I think, a trap. We need to think about the idea of museums as constantly evolving and trying to understand different dimensions of culture as they evolve and change and new forms emerge. As someone who makes multimedia works, I'm painfully aware of how difficult it is to show works within the context of contemporary museums.

I've heard this anecdote that MoMA's galleries were conceived by assessing the ability to move Richard Serra sculptures. So, the galleries are an articulation of space rooted in a specific moment in the 1960s when art had a physical presence that was in many ways monumental and inert. But now, these are the same spaces that are meant to exhibit multimedia or ephemeral works, and the museum is struggling to provide for the basic functions that are essential to their presentation, such as sound mitigation or variance in light levels, scale, or programmatic flow. So, what happens next? Our conception of the museum has to change. It has to adapt to the ways artists make work now.

SJ   One interesting typology to solve the problem of continually amassing work is Herzog & de Meuron's Schaulager and the storage building as a space for the display of art. In many ways, the lineage of the "archive as a space of display" was made quite prominent by the Menils and their idea of the "treasure room." This is a space where works are typically hidden away that is re-conceived as a space for looking at, learning from, and putting works together to study, both as an institution and with artists and visitors. I think what's so attractive about the ephemeral space of the storage depot is that it allows for a more ad hoc and episodic experience with art. This is perhaps less prevalent in the United States, but I think it's coming.

DH   I keep thinking about what MoMA or even the Fogg will look like in 100 years, after 100 more years of artists and collectors contributing works. At a certain point, MoMA will be the same size as Manhattan, and that's an impossibility.

STIRLING'S SKETCHES OF SACKLER

Drawing for the Arthur M. Sackler Museum, Color Study for Quincy Street Elevation, 1982.140.1

Drawing for the Arthur M. Sackler Museum, Color Study for Quincy Street Elevation, 1982.140.3.

DAVID HARTT & SHARON JOHNSTON WITH VLADIMIR GINTOFF

Drawing for the Arthur M. Sackler Museum, Color Study for Quincy Street Elevation, 1982.140.2.

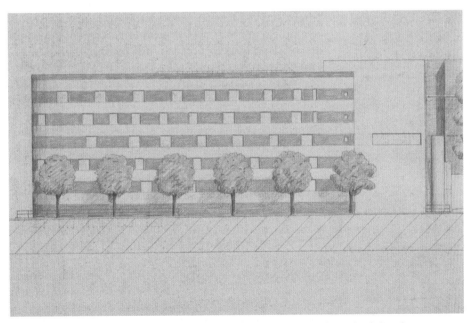

Drawing for the Arthur M. Sackler Museum, Color Study for Quincy Street Elevation, 1982.140.4.

STIRLING'S SKETCHES OF SACKLER

In many of the questions we're asking about repatriation, accountability, and the roles that museums play as repositories for our culture, what we're really asking for, I think, is a kind of opening up. I like the word "porosity." What happens when the museum is everywhere?

SJ   Yes, if some things come in and others go out, it's more of a responsive ecosystem that is not all one way anymore. The pandemic has also amplified an institutional desire for creating spaces not only for looking at and consuming art but also for participating in and learning about art. Learning spaces are increasingly driving the organization of institutions. How do you come together and talk about things beyond consuming them as an individual? I think that this paradigm is another example of the layers of everyday life slowly infiltrating what we expect from a museum. We're learning there, eating there, socializing there, and we're seeing art there too. On some levels, it's more prosaic, but perhaps it's also more profound because of how enmeshed the museum-going experience is in our everyday lives now. I don't know exactly where this leads, but it's moving beyond the idea of museums continually growing bigger as singular institutions.

DH   To end, I'd like to consider an example of the absolute failure of a cultural institution to understand the importance of a distributed idea of culture. In Chicago, one of the city agencies had commissioned a Kerry James Marshall painting. They decided to auction it off because of how expensive it was to insure, and it brought in 20-some million dollars. It went into private hands. There was another Kerry James Marshall painting that was made for the Percent-for-Art program for a library in a poor and underserved neighborhood. The city decided that it would auction that piece off as well. There was massive pushback from the neighborhood. Kerry James was very outspoken himself, and ultimately, the city decided not to sell the second painting.

      The Chicago case reminds me of scenarios like the Elgin Marbles, where artworks are removed because we don't understand their value in context. We don't understand the role that things play within specific communities. Our concept of the museum needs to be more distributed. Perhaps some museums have an agency that negotiates connections to things that are out in the community, but they also have this repository of artworks that, for whatever reason, no longer have a context.

John R. Stilgoe

with Kyle Winston

Sever Hall Graffito

On Fantasy and Education in Value

JOHN R. STILGOE   I'm a very early morning person. I come to work sometimes—well, this time of year, if I was coming to work—before daylight. Certainly in December.

KYLE WINSTON   Why so early?

JRS   It's because I'm the first person in my family to go to college, Kyle! And when I went to college, I realized there were much better prepared students. So, I was going to do what Thomas Jefferson said of John Adams, that for 50 years, he rose before the sun. I can do *that*. I get up every morning—the alarm is at 4:30 a.m.—and take the third Red Line train from Braintree to Boston.

KW   I first learned about this photo and its content, the graffito, in a virtual walking tour of Harvard Yard you gave about 10 years ago. You mention it very briefly. When did you take it?

JRS   Oh, it must have been 2004. The graffito is visible only in December at daybreak, when the light hits the wall just so. You can see there's some snow on the ground. The university has tried to clean it since, and it's made a good effort. In broad daylight, you can't see it.

KW   You noticed it early when you got to work?

JRS   In order to unlock Sever Hall, I have to use the accessible entrance, which is underneath the graffito. And when I come around the south end of Sever, sometimes I can see it. So, I photographed it with a film camera. And it's only because I get up early that I notice some things. And I get up early because I'm still trying … I mean, you can't slack off, right? I like the early morning. It's quiet and all the rest of it.
      I knew instantly what it was. I was in college when the National Guard killed those students.

KW   Did you discover it?

"Kent State 4 Dead" graffito on Harvard's Sever Hall. Photograph by John R. Stilgoe, 2004.

JOHN R. STILGOE WITH KYLE WINSTON

JRS   Yes. I had classes in the building when I got here to do my PhD. My predecessor, the late, great J. B. Jackson, had his office in Sever, so I had been looking at it for years. The buildings used to have ivy all over them. And there was a massive, remove-the-ivy effort circa 1980. So, the ivy came down and revealed the graffito. It was cleaned right away. But it's almost impossible to get the paint out of the brick. And they've really tried [*laughs*]. And they've *really tried* since it got on video.

KW   In my mind, this photo quite explicitly conjures many contemporary issues: protest, police violence, rioting, campus life (or lack thereof), subjects of incessant conversation today. How much does the content of the graffito matter to your image of it?

JRS   Not much. What intrigues me is how rarely people see it.
        Part of what I used to teach is that a great many brick buildings have painted signs on them. They fade over the decades, and when the light is right, you see them. I teach a seminar now that deals in part with fantasy being the fall of light on a place, which is not my idea but Ursula K. Le Guin's. And the difficulty is that most young people in a university, if they see low light, they are out in the late afternoon, not at dawn watching it. I've published on this: how Hollywood brought us the whole notion of the sun setting over the ocean.

KW   A few years ago, you wrote for the GSD student publication *Open Letters* (in which you cite Le Guin) about the role of fantasy in education. It's addressed to the Lords Griffin, the lionesque statues that used to adorn Hunt Hall and now occupy Gund Hall's vestibule. So, I'm wondering how you get into this, because fantasy seems to often target a certain "coming-of-age" audience. You wrote about its role in the 1970s as an emergent *way of knowing*, which in turn affected a generation.

JRS   Well, first, fantasy is not the imagination, and it's not reverie. It's another state. And it's been popular among adults since about 1900 when the Irish nobleman, Lord Dunsany, wrote a lot of it. It's a way for a lot of adults after 1900 to just toy with ideas. It's not imagination. It's not anywhere near as valuable. But after Tolkien, it became a way of toying with ideas that, you're right, often happen around adolescence, especially for children who can read well, smart kids, and this is not typically talked about in the public realm.
        So, part of what the fantasy seminar is about is preparing us for new life forms that we're going to create or that will

arrive, I don't know, from outer space or whatever. It does a lot. I'm finishing a piece now about what it's done to the appreciation and evaluation of public school buildings by kids, because the kids have read about and then seen in the Harry Potter movies Hogwarts—and it's pretty damn hard to make a public elementary school come anywhere near that.

KW   Are you suggesting architects of public schools can do better, or is this just another example of Hollywood establishing ideals?

JRS   Regulations govern so much of public-school architecture that no one blames architects. But fantasy emphasizes the limits of public-school architecture and what passes for public education.

KW   So, is it just an exercise to expand our understanding?

JRS   Fantasy drives the limits now. People discover something in fantasy and want it.

KW   I wanted to talk to you, John, in part, because your writing and even your position at the GSD seems novel and a bit quaint. There is a straightforwardness to your approach that many now take issue with, at least implicitly. That is, the extent to which "noticing" can be some claim on an objective landscape. And your writing does not hide from this. You write very personally, through, for example, what you've deemed the "prismatic function of remembered childhood landscapes." And from what I've learned thus far, you teach a similar scrutiny to your students, presumably leveraging their own memory. Is this fair?

JRS   Yes, fair … and it is exactly why so many AI and AR firms—and the venture capitalists behind them—contact me.

If you look to the right of the graffito, the horse chestnut leaves were not specified by H.H. Richardson. He left that to the masons to imagine. And this is a great building in part because the brickwork is extraordinary.

So, what you get is that this burgeoning genre is driving design because clients insist on it. What I've found is adults who are extremely powerful and like fantasy will ask landscape architects and architects to design the grounds and house for them based on some ideas they read. So, I start thinking about how often GSD alumni run into somebody with a load of money and a lot of ideas, which comes down to wanting something fantastical. That's why I teach the fantasy seminar: fantasy is a force.

But where I'm going with this is my undergraduates tell me they started to think first about light when they were reading fantasy novels. For example: firelight, candlelight, kerosene light. I've never seen whale-oil light … whale oil is hard to get, but I have seen gaslight, and I understand why nobody wanted to be seen by that! But all I'm telling you, Kyle, is that fantasy puts ideas into kids' heads often before they've hit puberty!

And the ideas develop not just in the heads of young people, who create computer games, but in a lot of other minds. Two of my former students have successfully sued architects, for example, who did not site their houses according to the contract documents. And one of the arguments in both cases was about the kitchen. The kitchen was to be oriented to a certain angle for the passage of the sun. These are women who have enormous power. And I listen to these

JOHN R. STILGOE WITH KYLE WINSTON

people! They want something they claim is better. Whether it's better, I don't know, but they want it.

KW　You seem to think of these issues more from the position of the client than the designers who you presumably teach—

JRS　You're talking to a man who has taught a lot of GSD students … but I've taught more developers. And they, the clients, are the people who make the real design decisions. Architects have to settle in and make the best of it. A landscape architect can at least tell a client, "Well, you're not going to have palm trees in northern New Jersey, so forget that, okay?"

A great many people have visceral responses to urban design that are never dealt with by urban designers unless a particular person is very powerful and can say, "I'm not having this!" And I'm curious about what developers tell me. If you expect educated, upscale, upwardly mobile women, for example, to do good work in a building, the building has to be "well-lit." Meaning, it should have natural light, and it should have, nowadays, LEDs that are properly color-balanced. And it probably should not have off-white walls. Women perform creatively best when there is some blue on the walls.

KW　Okay, okay. So, I want to get your reflection on something else. You mentioned Jefferson and his daily routine as inspiration for your own and also your predecessor J. B. Jackson. In a review in the *Harvard Design Magazine* from 1998, writer Mitchell Schwarzer discusses Jackson in relation to Jefferson in a manner that reminded me of your own:

KW　Wait, this is specific to women? Why?

JRS　It's biological. I mean, listen, if it's learned, nobody in sociology seems to know why; social psychologists don't seem to know. But the worst way to encourage creativity in women is to put down some gray wall-to-wall carpeting and paint everything off-white. And so, all you have to do, Kyle, is get out more! If you want to make people happier, particularly people who are blue-eyed, you'd get rid of fluorescent lights right away. I teach this and my students usually open their mouths and just stare at me.

Nobody wants to talk about this stuff. It's politically edgy, but it's the base of what I do. And I find myself fascinated with the fact that my students in Silicon Valley know all about it and employ it when they come up with the color palette for a computer game or something. My students in marketing research understand it. My students who are real estate developers are getting to the point where they believe the interior design is more important than what the architect does to the building.

I mean, when I started teaching in Sever, all the furniture was wood, and it was beautiful. And after the 1980 renovation

The America portrayed [by Jackson] … is absent the critical glance of psycho-analytic, Marxist, or semiotic theory, the essays conjure a country of Cyclopean dimensions and Odyssean wandering … [an] unpredictable freedom of the individual spirit and [of the] senses. As [Jackson] wrote: 'All that we can now do is produce landscapes for unpredictable men where the free and democratic intercourse of the Jeffersonian landscape can somehow be combined with the intense self-awareness of the solitary Romantic.' Landscape had to satisfy both functional demands and reflective aspirations— physiological and psychological requirements.

49

Griffin statue atop Harvard's now-demolished Hunt Hall, 1974.

it was gutted! There were original Richardson-designed desks in every classroom!

KW   Where did they go?

JRS   The contractor took them! I have the only Richardson-designed desk left! I bought it off the back of a truck and hired undergraduates to carry it to safety ... I thought, "What kind of a university ... " Well, anyway—

But we now have cheap tables with chrome legs and everything. In the seminar rooms, the beautiful big wooden oblong tables are gone. And I think to myself, "Okay, if you go to prep school in this country, you're highly unlikely to have plastic tables with chrome legs or tables covered in particle board, but if you go to public school, you get that."

The clash at Harvard that you guys think of as maybe race- or class-based is much more nuanced. I have seen students walk into my seminar room, particularly the women, just knock the back of their hand against the table, and say like, "What's this? I've come to Harvard, why do we have this junk?"

KW   Can you elaborate? Nuanced in what way?

JRS   Germany banned fan coil units years ago, but US architects still specify them. They make such a racket in my Sever classrooms that I must turn them off. Freshmen arriving at the College who have been taught that such devices indicate a

JOHN R. STILGOE WITH KYLE WINSTON

lack of concern for building occupants rightly wonder why Harvard permits them.

Discriminating in favor of quality illuminates not racial, ethnic, gender, and other trendy issues but sophisticated, long-term education in value. One undergraduate woman, now a venture capitalist underwriting AI firms, told me that architects specifying fan coil units "wear double-knit polyester clothes."

KW   That's funny, but are you suggesting our job is to then just be experts in these particular details?

JRS   A great many architects cannot name the component details on facades they intend to replace. They cannot explain the acoustic character of furniture, ventilation systems, elevators, etc.

KW In contrast, in a contemporary take on what's Jeffersonian, Mabel O. Wilson writes in her new book *Race and Modern Architecture* on the Virginia State Capitol Building, pointing out that the Jeffersonian wanderer is imbued with prejudices, as was, we all know, Jefferson himself:

KW   I know that many of my peers in the department of architecture do not want to practice in the traditional sense (so as to confront the consideration of what you describe). They go to school for the degree knowing or learning soon enough that the methods taught have value in a lot of other arenas as a liberal art, let's say, as a way of thinking. The details of buildings or specific qualities of interior spaces, as you describe, are often not, oddly enough, always of primary interest.

JRS   What are they going to do to earn their living?

KW   Content creation, maybe, user interface design, other jobs in academia, media, and tech.

In these … designs, the high ground, both natural and man-made, provided Jefferson the opportunity to architecturally reconcile the paradox between freedom and slavery by placing some of the slave dependencies beneath the main living spaces in rooms and passages hidden from view. This way, the white-columned Neoclassical buildings appeared to visitors as idyllic beacons of democratic values overlooking sublime nature unsullied by the presence of those spaces in which unsightly slaves toiled to make the land fertile and the lives of white citizens comfortable.

JRS   Okay. Let's assume that there was an alternative to the GSD where they could go and maybe learn something slightly different about content creation. Let's take the World Building Media Lab at USC, for example, which is taking students, my graduates, who are thinking about going to architecture school but interested in what you just said. So, why not go to a program that's focused on it? I mean, how do you create, for instance, the scenery of a computer game like *Resident Evil*? So, go to a graduate program that will teach you this! And these programs, I know, are competing with the GSD, but they're competing for students who, when they're sophomores or juniors, are connected enough to find out. Then, they decide, "Do I really want to go to a professional school and kind of acquire what I'm going to do but not design buildings? Or should I go to a school that is focused on what I want to do?"

51

JRS   This is a hell of a conversation to have with a graduate student .... But I'll tell you, Kyle, I've thought an awful lot about GSD students not wanting to go out and design buildings or landscapes. And so, I'll tell you a brief history of it: In the 1990s, GSD studio faculty were very upset because the top students did not want to be teaching assistants. They could go to East Cambridge and proofread computer games for 50 bucks an hour. The money was just too good. And then, students started dropping out to go do video games. And that was all fine and dandy, until all of a sudden architecture students weren't needed anymore. What the companies in East Cambridge wanted were undergraduates who had a couple of CS courses and could not only proofread but could, just on a sidebar, write down what the correction should be. Now, I have a lot of Harvard College alumni who are venture capitalists who invest in content generation, and I think the time of architects working in entertainment is going away because there are now people who have different degrees coming in.

And where I'm ending this is that after 9/11, computer game companies that produced war games told the Pentagon, "We can create training exercises. So, we can show you real landscapes in the Middle East and help your soldiers." And they awarded contracts without public bidding. They have become the military simulation and training industry. In the beginning, if you were a landscape architect who was willing to sign on, it was golden. This is the landscape now, and this is how the landscape will look when the Air Force takes out the bridge before you get there. This is a whole world out there.

KW   While this might be an obvious industry where our skills translate, I imagine you can sense why mostly liberal young designers might be a bit reluctant to engage with defense contracting.

JRS   Yes, I sense that, but other designers engage enthusiastically. Left-leaning professionals (newspaper reporters and other news-media types) now earn far less relatively than they did 25 years ago. That is worth remembering ...

It's easy to think about the GSD as a bubble. You're in Gund all day long. You figure, "This is what we're all doing." I don't know if you wander off to conferences of video game designers or the like, but you should. The key is not to find out what those people are doing. The key is to figure out where they've come from.

KW   I imagine Wilson would agree there is nothing obviously free or democratic in the Jeffersonian landscape, as Jackson suggests. So how do we reconcile our own prismatic lenses with these historical conditions? Can we?

JRS   Presentism corrodes any retrospect analysis of anything: all historians earning PhDs in any kind of history learn to scorn it. Ascribing moral, aesthetic, and other values of the present to the past proves puerile. Noticing, looking—not searching— encourages individual acuity, thought, and enterprise. Few theorists of the American landscape spend much time exploring it firsthand. If no one notices a graffito, theorists cannot theorize about such, nor can AI and AR work their peculiar magic on it.

Rashid bin Shabib
& Gareth Doherty

with Vladimir Gintoff

Tange's Drawings of St. Mary's

On Places and Perceptions

RASHID BIN SHABIB   When did we first meet, Gareth?

GARETH DOHERTY   Well, I'm curious to hear what you think.

RBS   I think it was years ago, and we were communicating over email. Then, I think we were reintroduced through Mohsen [Mosta-favi, the former dean of the Graduate School of Design] and finally met for the first time in Dubai. Is that right, Gareth?

GD   Kind of, but I have a slightly different version of the story. I was in Dubai with Steven Caton and Nader Ardalan. We were spending a month doing fieldwork in the Gulf about contemporary urbanization, and I recall meeting at the Burj Khalifa. I remember this very rushed event with lots of people, and everyone was agitated, and you were very busy. Then, I think we all jumped in a car or taxi and drove to the Shelter because you guys had the Shelter in Dubai back then.

RBS   Yes, now I remember. It must've been 2006 or 2007 when we took over the old warehouse in the middle of the industrial area Al Quoz. Now it has become a popular place for galler-ists and designers and that OMA project, but then we were just kids from Dubai, only 22, and we took over one of the old warehouses and converted it into a kind of civic space for cultural and educational activities. Then, all of a sudden, it became such a dynamic venue that was connecting the city to the broader world of design.

VLADIMIR GINTOFF   I was eager to hear your origin story, so I'm glad I didn't even have to ask. Rashid, regarding your early days, I'm wondering if we can talk about how *Brownbook* started and why it ended after 67 issues. For those who don't know about this project, *Brownbook* was a bimonthly magazine that you coedited with your twin brother Ahmed focused on urban and architectural stories of the Middle East and North Africa.

RBS *Brownbook* also began when we were around 21 or 22. What we wanted to do was look at design representation of the region from an inside perspective. This was at a time when the city was becoming very popular with franchising and thinking about itself, "How can we bring the world to Dubai?" We were thinking the opposite—how we could bring Dubai to the world. Once we created the Shelter, *Brownbook* came as a natural extension because we were not only interested in Dubai, we were interested in this form of representation across the world.

Somehow the magazine managed to stumble its way through the first few years and then formed a unique identity as it kept growing. It was exciting to have the readership of the magazine branch out, not just to locals but to people in, say, Dearborn, Michigan, where there's an Arab community. And they would say, "This magazine touches us in a way that other publications haven't." One of the major elements that I feel made the magazine a success was the constant message of positivity.

It might sound a bit cliché in a broader sense, but I have chosen specific words because, in reality, we live in a region that's extremely turbulent, and when you create a magazine that addresses a unified presentation of the Middle East, it makes everyone super proud. And all the more for the fact that we could generate unity through a focus on diversity. I'm very emotional about a lot of the energy that was put into it. But, as with anything, I think at some point the magazine reached a level where we felt it had served its purpose. And, 12 years into it, the region had changed, the world had changed, and publishing had changed. Ahmed and I decided to think proactively. It wasn't that we couldn't continue to sustain the magazine but that we could decide when it was time to call it quits.

VG Rashid, I believe you said in your AA [Architectural Association School of Architecture] lecture on Dubai that it's a part of the world we have a lot of information about but don't yet fully understand. The sentiment seemed like an opportunity to discuss your own work as juxtaposed with Gareth's, as you both promote local strategies to offer insight on conditions that might otherwise be overlooked. Can you each describe how models for careful observation inform your roles as urban thinkers?

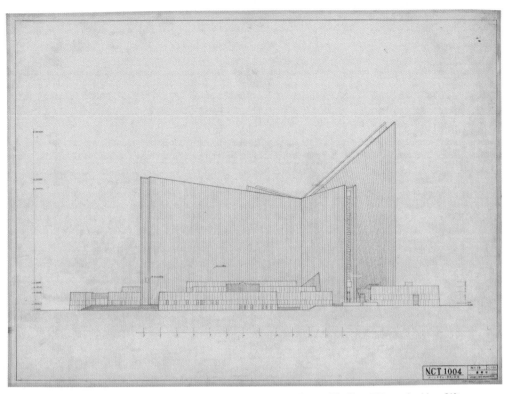

Kenzō Tange, St. Mary's Cathedral, Tokyo. The Kenzō Tange Archive, Gift of Takako Tange, 2011. Folder A052. Courtesy of the Frances Loeb Library, Harvard University Graduate School of Design.

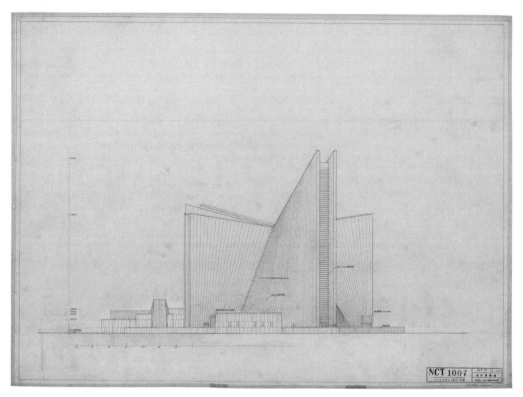

Kenzō Tange, St. Mary's Cathedral, Tokyo. The Kenzō Tange Archive, Gift of Takako Tange, 2011. Folder A052. Courtesy of the Frances Loeb Library, Harvard University Graduate School of Design.

RASHID BIN SHABIB & GARETH DOHERTY WITH VLADIMIR GINTOFF

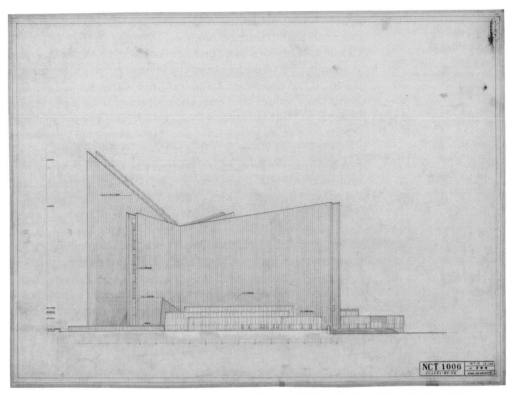

Kenzō Tange, St. Mary's Cathedral, Tokyo. The Kenzō Tange Archive, Gift
of Takako Tange, 2011. Folder A052. Courtesy of the Frances Loeb Library,
Harvard University Graduate School of Design.

GD   I think that in order to understand the world we live in, we also need to understand how people relate to that world. So, it's not just objects but objects in relation to each other and to people. And to understand these relationships, I think, it's helpful, if not essential, to spend time with people to understand their values and how they interact with a particular landscape. That landscape includes architecture, it includes people, and it includes time and environmental processes. It's really quite complex. But it takes time to understand that complex landscape, and you have to embed yourself in it, not just observe but participate, work in, walk through, and understand it, and talk with people. That's what I've been doing, mostly in Bahrain, but a little bit in other Gulf States as well.

RBS   Back to the notion of identity, I think a sense of belonging has become so central to Ahmed and me, given that we are based in a city like Dubai. In a lot of our research, collective memory and shared memory become vessels that are so foundational and essential. And objects—I mean physical artifacts or buildings—have somehow become less of a priority. Instead, ecology has moved up on our ladder of consideration.

GD   You have this very distinctive perspective on Dubai because most of the writing about the city is by foreigners, like me, who come and observe and take the role of the outsider writing about the other. And yet, you're from Dubai and you have this insider perspective. It's like being an insider and outsider at the same time because you're bringing in an academic perspective. The anthropologist Lila Abu-Lughod describes it as being a "halfie," you're half in and you're half out. I think that allows you a fantastic perspective from which to view Dubai and the landscape.

RBS   In every critique about Dubai, some points are valid, but there are a lot of things that are very myopic and possibly misleading, things that choose to show one part of a very complex, long history. I think there's always an immediate reaction of trying to fill that void of information with a particular perspective, but there hasn't yet been a definitive text or body of work that does the city justice or paints a complete picture.

VG   Do you think that might have to do with it still being a relatively young place? The city's port has a much longer history, but Dubai as an international city is relatively new.

60

RBS There's a lot of cosmopolitanism, and there are truths to the city that people have yet to see, or the information has yet to be presented to the world in a very honest and brave way. The reason why I say "brave" is because if you look at Dubai in the context of the region and if you look at the volatility there, the way the city has been able to weather itself and create a sense of life and place for so many people is worthy of a level of braveness that's yet to be presented to the world, minus all its imperfections.

  I am always channeling the energy of my grandfather, who is 95. He says, "No matter how we've progressed, when I was a kid, I ate fish and curry, and today I still eat fish and curry." This is a kind of a metaphor for him, even if he's living in a house with lights, electricity, and everything else. There's this humble and honest perspective at his core, a perspective that hasn't yet been shared with the world.

  Anything you want to add, Gareth?

GD Nothing, except that I agree with you about Dubai, more or less. A lot of the writing is sensationalist, and there's a certain tone that's not entirely helpful because people … There are many different constituencies in Dubai that make up the city that are usually left out of the descriptions of the city, and this is an important dimension.

VG Shifting back to ecology, Rashid, could you talk about the *falaj* research that you and Ahmed have been working on? For those who don't know, falaj refers to ancient irrigation tactics used across the Arabian Peninsula.

RBS The project began around 2016, and Gareth was someone we used as a bouncing board, someone to share ideas back and forth with. With the falaj research, we were interested in ecology but specifically water sustainability. The water table across the Gulf is actually extremely high. If you dig past the surface, you immediately hit water, albeit water that is a bit brackish. So, the research wasn't about if there's water in the Gulf but rather about the quality of the water and how you channel it. This led us to study aquifers and the falaj systems, which are intrinsically linked to regional notions of oases. There was a lot of research that we did around that, which led to an exhibition at the London Design Biennale, and we also published a book with EPFN [École Polytechnique Fédérale de Lausanne] that was connected to our research on

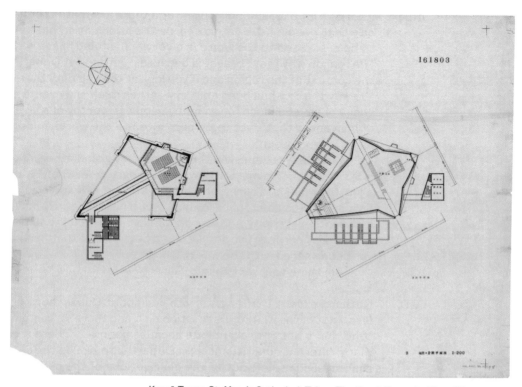

161803

Kenzō Tange, St. Mary's Cathedral, Tokyo. The Kenzō Tange Archive, Gift of Takako Tange, 2011. Folder A052. Courtesy of the Frances Loeb Library, Harvard University Graduate School of Design.

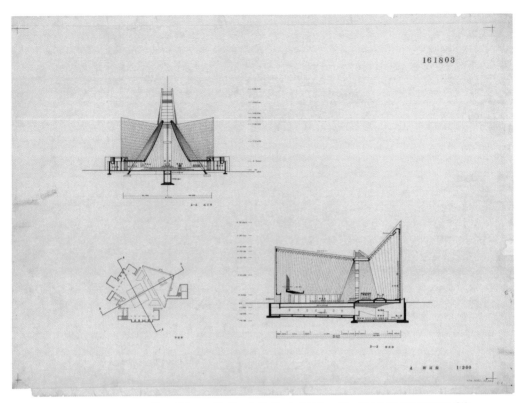

161803

Kenzō Tange, St. Mary's Cathedral, Tokyo. The Kenzō Tange Archive, Gift
of Takako Tange, 2011. Folder A052. Courtesy of the Frances Loeb Library,
Harvard University Graduate School of Design.

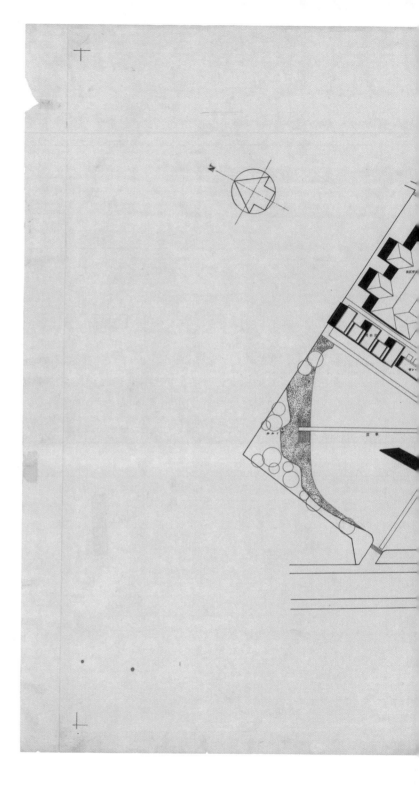

RASHID BIN SHABIB & GARETH DOHERTY WITH VLADIMIR GINTOFF

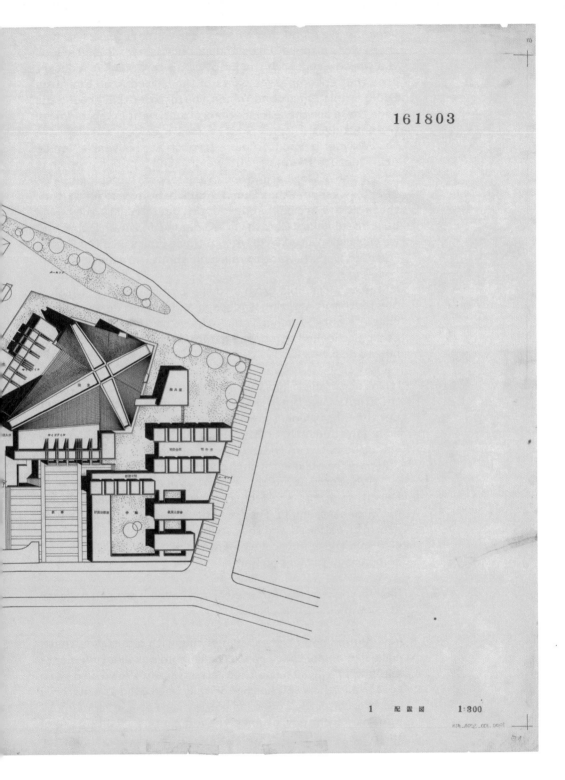

161803

1 配置図 1:300

sabkhas. We found that where these water reserves existed, there were also salt lakes and salt plains parallel to them. If you were to research the Empty Quarter, which is a desert area that encompasses parts of the United Arab Emirates, Saudi Arabia, Oman, and Yemen, you discover that around the sand there are these formations of salt, right in the middle of the emptiness.

We just presented our research at this year's Venice Architecture Biennale, and we created a publication that focuses on ecological and urban aspects of the sabkhas. A lot of people assume that Dubai, Abu Dhabi, and so forth, that these cities were built in the desert, but, in reality, they were built on salt lakes. Gareth visited Ahmed and me in Dubai, and we were so excited to drive him three hours into the Empty Quarter. Gareth, want to talk a bit about the experience?

GD   It was an incredible drive into the Empty Quarter, which is filled with this amazing landscape and doesn't deserve being called "empty." Rashid, I think you've said it looks like snow, but it also looked to me like craters on the moon. I don't know how to describe it.

RBS   I think one of the things that strikes anybody that's ever visited the Empty Quarter is that we're all familiar with the desert, but the Empty Quarter is not just a desert. There are these huge sand dunes that can go up to 20, 30, 40 meters high, and you drive between these huge formations and feel so small. When you're walking through the flats your shoes fill with salt.

What strikes me about sabkhas is actually exactly what Gareth said, that something so complex could ever hold the notion of being empty. They're actually very much alive. They're a form of wetlands, and they sequester carbon. Scholars have also said the ecological elements of sabkhas are the closest comparison to Mars on Earth.

VG   Rashid, you're also interested in how salt can be used to generate new building materials?

RBS   Yes, Ahmed and I are experimenting with alternative materials, like brine, that are extracts from desalination plants and finding ways to use them structurally. We've also been researching how salt has historically been used as a material within architecture. For example, Hassan Fathy, a very famous Egyptian architect, studied the indigenous architecture of the Siwa Oasis in northwest Egypt near the Libyan border. There, they use a material called *karshif* made of mud, salt, and minerals from the lake, which creates a binder that can act structurally.

The publication also looked at other Western modern architects who experimented with salt. At the 1934 exhibition *Deutsches Volk, Deutsche Arbeit* in Berlin, Mies presented walls made from coal and salt as architecture, which considered German industrial prowess. Philip Johnson also used salt-glazed bricks at the Kline Biology Tower at Yale, which opened in 1966. In Japan, too, Togo Murano used salt-glazed tiles to create textures in his buildings.

Shifting to sabkhas specifically, Cedric Price proposed a project in Abu Dhabi in 1973 called Water Wall. This project was a beautiful extension, almost Fun Palace-esque, but he was building on a sabkha, even though he made no reference to it. And Oscar Niemeyer as well. He was one of the first people to propose a project on Al Lulu Island in Abu Dhabi, and he wasn't aware that he was building on a sabkha too. So, it's very interesting that even though these architects were technologically savvy and had an artistic approach to what they did, they were so disconnected from the context. Maybe that's unfair. It's more likely the science just wasn't established enough yet for them to comprehend the ecology of where they were building.

VG I think this is the antithesis of what Gareth works on and teaches at the GSD, which are ways to achieve an embodied engagement with one's contexts. Gareth, correct me if I'm wrong, but courses like "Design Anthropology: Objects, Landscape, and Cities" or "Landscape Fieldwork: People, Politics, Practices" emphasize how to achieve deeply informed perspectives, don't they?

GD Well, I mean, they're based on the premise that through the embodied engagement of landscape fieldwork, we can understand human practices in a way that can help us be better designers. I should add that the course I'm currently teaching on landscape fieldwork is affiliated with the Critical Landscapes Design Lab at the GSD. The lab functions on two questions: How can designers work in societies that are not their own with respect and deference to others' values and ways of life? And what can we learn from societies without formal design disciplines, so we avoid transporting and superimposing a Western model onto other environments? The lab is involved in various projects that bring us to other understandings of landscape, which can help us be better designers here and there wherever here and there are, if that makes sense.

VG   On the subject of strategies and their applications, what brought you to Bahrain?

GD   Ethnographers rely a lot on chance, and I ended up in Bahrain by chance. I was invited to teach a workshop there, but I didn't really know at the time where Bahrain was. I thought it was near Indonesia. When I got there, I was totally amazed in just the three days that I spent there. I arrived in Bahrain during a dust storm, and it persisted for the entire time. The whole landscape became beige, including the sky and the atmosphere. I became intrigued that there appeared to be a fascination with the construction of green spaces in this arid, beige environment. In Bahrain, there's this obsession with constructing these really super lush spaces, which contrast with the beige environment. This intersected with my doctoral work at the GSD with Hashim Sarkis, and I was already interested in ideas of landscape urbanism and the projective aspects of ethnography.

    I noticed that in Bahrain a lot of the green space predated the development of buildings. People would build landscapes before building their houses. I became interested in that conceptually and wanted to know what the value of landscape was in Bahrain and what infrastructures were required to maintain it. I ended up going back to Bahrain the following year when I was invited to teach another workshop. It was then that I decided to focus on this place for my doctoral work. At the time, I realized I would have to spend a protracted period living there to construct my data because there are so few books on the landscape of Bahrain.

    The following year, I spent my time walking through the country. But it was walking in order to talk, right? So every time I'd walk, I'd try to observe and record my interactions with the landscape. And through talking with people, I realized that they had a very different understanding of landscape than I had because I was importing my own kind of Western idea of landscape. As I came around to being more sympathetic to the Bahraini categories of landscape, I realized that they understood it through the lens of color. So, it was the contrast of the constructed green with an indigenous beige. With that, I began to focus more on color itself as being representative of landscape in a Bahraini context and how Bahrainis see landscape.

VG   I read an interview where you said each hour of fieldwork should be accompanied by four hours of reflection on what you had seen. Could you talk about your methods and strategies a bit?

GD   Well, I mean, that's a rule of thumb, that for every hour you spend in the field, it takes four hours to interpret it. And you can interpret that hour through many different means, through writing, through sketching ... but the point is, it's not just what you see, it's also the interpretation of what you see. I think that's a really critical point. How do I do it? Well, it depends on the site, really.

VG   With your role in the Critical Landscapes Design Lab and your being on the steering committee of Harvard's Center for Middle Eastern Studies, how do you hope to shape the GSD's connections to the Gulf and the Middle East more broadly?

GD   Well, one of the aims of the lab is the production of knowledge, right? And there are huge parts of the world, including the Arabian Peninsula, that we don't have that much knowledge about. There's the Empty Quarter, for instance. When we look at a map of the world, we see there are many regions that don't really factor into our design discourse. One of the responsibilities we have is to produce knowledge that will challenge us and help us to respect and understand other societies better.
      The lab is affiliated with the Center for Middle Eastern Studies because we have a focus on the Arabian Peninsula, but we're also working in West Africa, Brazil, and other post-colonial societies. I think there's a lot that we can learn both from those societies and also about how to practice in them. I'm often shocked by what landscape architects design in the Arabian Peninsula, for instance, because it's designed for a Western context and not for the people there.
      I'm sorry, but I have to go in a minute because I was meant to be in another meeting a little while ago ...

VG   Rashid, do you also have to go?

RBS   I'm happy to continue.

GD   Rashid, thank you for including me in this conversation. It was very nice to see you both. We'll be in touch.

VG   Rashid, let's switch subjects to Kenzō Tange. I want to talk specifically about the suite of drawings of St. Mary's Cathedral. The project is somewhat unique as Tange wasn't a Christian when he designed the church in 1964, but he became one later in life, I think just two years before his death.

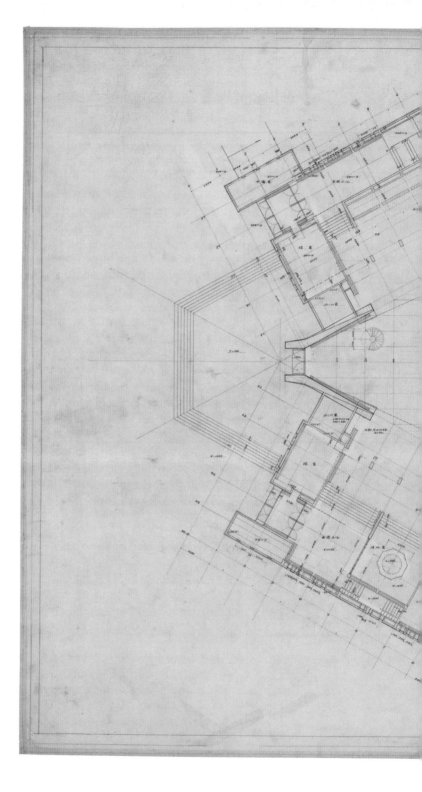

Kenzō Tange, St. Mary's Cathedral, Tokyo. The Kenzō Tange Archive, Gift of Takako Tange, 2011. Folder A052. Courtesy of the Frances Loeb Library, Harvard University Graduate School of Design.

70

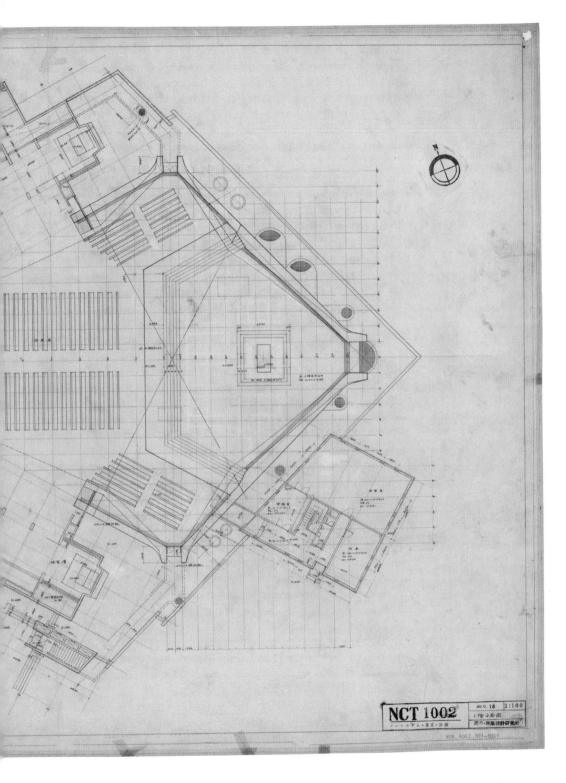

NCT 1002

RBS   Maybe I can tell you the story about my visit to St. Mary's.
        I should mention that Ahmed and I are very interested in
        Tange's research around mosques. I think one of the excep-
        tional qualities of Tange's architecture is that there's this
        inherent spiritual quality to his buildings, regardless of if
        they have a religious function. Naturally, on a visit to Japan,
        Ahmed, his wife, and I decided to go to St. Mary's, and coin-
        cidentally, it was a Sunday during mass. It was unbelievable.
        I don't know how we didn't put it together, but of course on
        Sunday the church has mass. So we went, and it's a little bit
        out of the regular of places that we hang out in. But we took a
        taxi, entered the church, and somehow the minute we walked
        in we saw a full house. Here we are, three Arabs, two men and
        a woman, that are dark-skinned walking in. We must have been
        perceived as something quite dramatic being ushered into
        this whole process.
            I can say that for me, particularly, it was such a moving
        experience, without a doubt, between the cathedral's archi-
        tecture and how well the space was being used and occupied.
        It's beautiful, and it amplified everything that was meant to
        be spiritual.

VG   Returning to *Brownbook* for a moment and considering ideas
        of legacy, the magazine profiled over 200 cities and featured
        interviews with more than 500 people. Do any particular arti-
        cles or full issues of the magazine stand out to you as what
        you imagine the legacy of the project will be?

RBS   For me, I think the magazine was an attempt to show the
        world a region that has a sense of unity despite immense
        diversity. I think that was something that we were trying to
        show ourselves, more so than talking to other people. It was a
        means of saying that we have so much more in common than
        we're led to believe. As an example, we did this whole issue on
        Constantine, Algeria, this fourth-tier city in the mountains
        where Oscar Niemeyer designed a beautiful campus, incred-
        ible architecture. By juxtaposing this context with a city like
        Grenoble, the feature we did revealed a shared quality of life
        and values of architecture and education. The two emphasize
        modes of existence that I think permeate across the region
        more so than we're led to believe. And I think this is the miscon-
        ception that we're trying to tackle.
            The whole magazine, too, was this effort against time to
        somehow audit all of these different topics: these people, living
        and deceased; these places, cities that still exist and others

that have been demolished. It was a way just to take account. We aren't the first to do this and won't be the last.

VG   Do you think you'll continue to focus on research and publishing, or could you imagine having a practice that combines these investigations with an actual architecture office?

RBS   I feel like we've dedicated more than a decade to looking at an important chapter that informs identity across the region. Whether it's migration, diaspora, whatever it is, we looked at it in the context of cities. We really put so much effort into that. Now, we're focusing on the more imminent challenge that will consume the coming generations. For us, this isn't our relationship to climate justice or climate change or building sustainably. What we're really preoccupied with is our relationship to and within nature. As we draw down this whole important investigation of identity with *Brownbook*, which is still very close to our hearts, Ahmed and I see a more imminent and important role within ecology, which is something we should all be putting our energy into. We're still focused on the region but in a different capacity to figure out what can and should endure.

Malkit Shoshan

with Emma Lewis

Missionary, UN, and Tuareg Tents

On Domestic Infrastructure and Liberating the Imagination

EMMA LEWIS   Let's talk about tents. You've shared a number of photographs and images of them with me. Why do you find them compelling and what do they represent?

MALKIT SHOSHAN   My interest derives from field research and a first encounter I had in Mali. When I landed at Modibo Keita International Airport in Bamako at night, I was picked up by a group of Dutch officers who accompanied me in a white UN van to a small UN transit camp built and operated by Swedish and Dutch peacekeepers. The camp is named Midgard, after an Old Norse tale in which Midgard is the wall around the world that the gods constructed from the first man's body.

Malkit Shoshan is transforming a research and design project she began in 2007 into the book *BLUE: Architecture of UN Peacekeeping Missions*, scheduled to be published in fall 2021 by Actar. It is designed in collaboration with Irma Boom and includes case studies in Mali.

Midgard is close to the airport, and it's surrounded by sandbags, a fence, and watchtowers. Inside the base, there are modular structures sized to fit into standard containers and tents. Upon arrival, I was directed to my lodging space for the following days—a tent.

EL   What were your impressions of that space?

MS   The tent itself felt very solid: it was attached to a concrete floor, had electric wires, and two air conditioners hanging on the tents' sides next to light switches. Strangely, it didn't feel like a tent. It was solid and grounded, like the entire camp. Although the UN presence in Mali was referred to as temporary, it looked, felt, and was operationally extremely permanent.

In the camp, I noticed two types of tents. One type is for people in transit, the missions' brief visitors or peacekeepers en route to other bases in the region. These are smaller and more tired looking. The other type is for those deployed by the mission and stationed at the base for longer periods. These are larger, newer, and golden,and their interiors resembled small apartments.

Exterior of UN peacekeepers' tents at Midgard, a UN transit camp in Mali.

MALKIT SHOSHAN WITH EMMA LEWIS

Interior of a tent at Midgard, a UN transit camp in Mali.

EL   I'm looking at one of the photos you took of two people watch-
      ing television inside of a tent. It does look like an apartment
      interior. After your time in Midgard, what came next?

MS   After visiting the UN base, I traveled across Mali. The coun-
      try is staggeringly beautiful, and it has a rich history where
      sedentary and nomadic cultures intersect. Nomadic people
      and their domestic infrastructures are part of the landscape
      and cultural history of the region. In the north, nomadic tribes
      move between the Sahara and cities along the edge of the
      desert seasonally.
          There is a beautiful symbiosis between human habitats
      and nature that we're not used to here in the West or in
      the Global North. The UN base's engineering logic and rigid-
      ity, which is contingent on security regulation, protocols,
      global supply chains, and procurement politics, looked very
      foreign here.
          I noticed the striking difference between the environ-
      ments created by the UN tentage designers and by the locals.
      These intertwined landscapes in the Sahel, composed of differ-
      ent cultures and lifestyles, became extremely apparent at the
      scale of the tent—its architecture, materiality, technology,
      politics, and aesthetics.

A model Tuareg tent. Courtesy of FAST/Malkit Shoshan.

EL   After leaving Mali, how did your thinking about these juxta-positions between the UN tent design and locally-designed tents evolve?

MS   I came across the wonderful work of Labelle Prussin, an anthropologist researching nomadic life in sub-Saharan Africa, particularly the Tuareg people in western Africa. Her book *African Nomadic Architecture: Space, Place and Gender*, in which she attempts to introduce nomadic structures in Africa into the Western architectural cannon, was of particular interest.

Labelle identifies missionary tents as political and institutional symbols, in contrast to nomadic tents, which she identifies as homes, places of social reproduction and the complexities of family life. She ascribes the rich variety of tent and nomadic camp designs to women. The men often travel for work, leaving the responsibility of the nomadic settlement design and management to the women of the community. In comparison, the missionary tents and camp have a reductive engineering logic and are designed, according to her, by men.

EL   I'd love to speak more about tent design, but first, could you share more about the political and social history of the Tuareg in Mali?

MS   Yes, I can. The conflict in Mali can be traced back to the long history of European colonization and control over the African continent and its resources. In Mali and sub-Saharan Africa, national borders were drawn relatively recently, after the World Wars. In doing so, international powers recognized some nations while others were left behind and excluded from that process, like the Tuareg, the Saharan nomads. Their ongoing rebellion and plea for self-determination has been silenced and ignored by the international community and the United Nations.

The Gaddafi regime in Libya offered some recognition for the Tuareg men by allowing them access to employment and sustained income. After Gaddafi's downfall, the Tuareg men fled back to the desert to join their families. However, they quickly realized that their livelihoods were strained. The climate crises turned seasons unbearably hot and dry and made the desert of sub-Saharan Africa uninhabitable. At the same time, new international security regimes following 9/11 and the War on Terror, impacted Africa and prevented the Tuareg from moving freely in the desert and accessing cities along the Niger River, as they historically had done when in need of water, food, and employment. They reenacted

Nomadic tent model, based on *African Nomadic Architecture: Space, Place, and Gender*, by Labelle Prussin. Courtesy of FAST/Malkit Shoshan.

MALKIT SHOSHAN WITH EMMA LEWIS

their rebellion and their appeals for self-determination and captured territories in northern Mali by force. In response, the international community adopted a resolution to initiate a new peacekeeping mission in Mali.

EL   Thanks for helping me contextualize this. I'm wondering about tents as spaces conceptualized and actualized by women. What makes the tents designed by nomadic women, particularly the Tuareg women, unique?

MS   The Tuareg are one of the most ancient nomadic tribes in the Sahara and sub-Saharan regions, and their lives are suffused with the landscape and nature. There is a sense when you look at these spaces that the body and nature are one, and that home is an extension of the body. They carry their homes with them, assembling and disassembling them as needed. This domestic infrastructure has a very low environmental footprint. The tribes have domesticated animals, and sheep's wool is woven into cloth that is used as a soft wall or a carpet covering the soil. When the temperature drops, another layer of camel or sheepskin is wrapped around the tent to further isolate and regulate the temperature inside.

New tents are erected during marriage. In the marriage ceremony, the bride arrives with the center pole of the tent, called a *dobal*. This is the main column of the tent, and through-out the woman's life, she continues developing and adding to this tent. It has to be relatively easy to disassemble because everything is constantly on the move, but as a family grows old, the tent becomes more ornamented and layered. I like the thought of a tent growing as an inseparable part of the woman's body and life, and that the elements of a tent tell its story. The tent, in fact, is also called "womb" by the Tuareg in Tamashek, their native language.

EL   What do you imagine as a potential future for the UN mission tents? Are you optimistic that they might evolve to become more sustainable and lower impact?

MS   The UN tents provide housing for peacekeepers, and they are emblematic of the UN's institutional history and culture. After the 2008 financial crisis, the UN had to restructure its economic organization. One of the outcomes of this was the delegation of mission production to the private sector, which increased the dependency on global supply chains. It inflated the budgets and environmental footprints of UN missions, as well as the size of their tents. More than half of the UN's

81

17th-century European missionary tent model, based on *African Nomadic Architecture: Space, Place, and Gender*, by Labelle Prussin. Courtesy of FAST/ Malkit Shoshan.

carbon emissions are generated by its peacekeeping missions. Given the climate crisis, the UN must rethink its wasteful and harmful practices. We need to shift the paradigm and work toward just, environmentally sustainable systems.

EL   Right. How are you involved in this work of shifting the paradigm, especially within an organization as historically and politically complex as the UN? What's the role of design in this process?

MS   Through my design practice FAST (Foundation for Achieving Seamless Territory), we engaged UN agencies in conversations about change. We collaborated with policy institutions to develop reports and lobbied the UN with the support of a few member states that were eager to reform UN agencies and their missions. So far, one of our reports has been adopted by high-level policymakers at the UN.

The UN is a hugely complicated organization; it is bureaucratic, siloed, and not very responsive to change. Design helped us throughout the process, especially in liberating the imagination of policymakers, military engineers, diplomats, and policy institutions to imagine what is possible beyond the scope of their mandates and protocols. Adding a spatial perspective to the discussions around missions was especially effective. Although the change is incremental, I find the process fascinating and hopeful.

EL   I'm interested in design's role in liberating the imagination, and in the question of how patterns of action can shift even within large, highly bureaucratic institutions such as the UN. I agree that if there isn't some intention and effort to point out what else might be possible then nothing else *will* be possible.

MS   The spaces and places in which UN missions take place are some of the most impoverished in the world. In northern Mali, resources are scarce. Famine, extreme poverty, disease, and various forms of violence are of daily concern to the locals. To engage in activism, one must deploy a multitude of practices and strategies, one of which is to converse with those who may not be entirely in line with you ethically and morally.

We need to find ways to engage and empower people, such as UN policymakers, with the tools and ideas to help them start moving toward different institutional forms. We need to find ways to liberate resources from powerful institutions and move them toward those in need.

83

EL   Could you tell me about a moment of change being actualized or a moment that made you feel hope?

MS   At one of the bases I visited in Mali, a UN subcontractor hired a local builder to construct a large outdoor pergola as an extension to the base dining room. The builder arrived with a group of ten people and assembled a gorgeous, straw roof. It was local; it was an ad hoc decision bypassing all protocols that created a beautiful structure suitable to the local climate and culture and created a few job opportunities for the local people. This project is an example of a practice that can be replicated, and it's the kind of moment we pull out, magnify, and point out to the UN. We look for precedents and specific, quantifiable situations that can be used to support institutional change. It is however a complex matrix, matching field findings with policy opportunities and beginning to lobby for new approaches.

EL   Do you have advice for designers who want to use design as a mechanism to enact justice?

MS   Follow your own path: consider what direction you want to move in, where you want to invest your energy, and what you are able to do. I do think it's important to ask yourself, "How do I make a living if I work in a space that has no market incentives?" It requires a lot of perseverance and belief in what you're doing. Personally, I am glad about pursuing a practice at the intersection of design and activism. People are very eager to follow this path. They need to understand the cost. At FAST, every project starts with fundraising and every project depends on building trust. As designers, we can play a key role in the struggle for justice.

       Architecture production is contingent on power and finance. The construction industry is at the heart of the neoliberal market, capitalism, and financial speculation, and this notion is overwhelming. But what if the disciplines of spatial design and architecture are transformed into public service? There are so many exciting examples of practices that are working relentlessly toward empowerment and equity. This is not an individual struggle for a more just society but a collective one.

84

Irma Boom

with Kimberley Huggins

The Vergilius Vaticanus

On Peace of Mind

IRMA BOOM   Hey! You were at the lecture I gave at Harvard?

KIMBERLEY HUGGINS   Yes, I was! The way you spoke about your work was so joyful and freeing. It really struck a chord with students. I found out afterward that you were doing research in the Vatican Library and have been curious about your experience since.

IB   You know, when I gave that lecture, I flew in from Rome.

KH   I didn't realize the two overlapped. How did your time in Rome begin?

IB   A few years ago, I got an email from the American Academy's office in New York inviting me to become a resident of the American Academy in Rome. The email just read, "Do you want to become a resident of the American Academy in Rome?" So, I simply answered, "Yes." This was around 2016, way ahead of my time there, and then at some point, I found myself on a plane to Rome.

The American Academy is, as you know, for American Prix de Rome winners, but it turns out that they can invite non-Americans every year for about six to eight weeks as well. I ultimately arrived at this incredible Academy building in Rome with only my laptop and some of my books. They offered me this fantastic studio—big windows, lots of light. The Academy is an interdisciplinary environment: scientists, painters, photographers, musicians, architects, landscape architects and designers in all kinds of fields—and a bookmaker!

I was certain that I would have responsibilities after I arrived, but the director said that I was their guest and free to do what I liked. So, I did. I began visiting some of Rome's many great libraries, like Biblioteca Angelica and Biblioteca Casanatense. I rented a bike because the Academy is on the

The Vatican Apostolic Library (Biblioteca Apostolica Vaticana), informally known as the Vat or BAV, was the vision of Pope Nicholas V, who reigned from 1447 to 1455. He intended to create a knowledge resource for public and scholarly use at the geographical heart of the Roman Catholic Church. Now, centuries later, the collection holds a trove of writings at the core of the Western tradition. The library is sited within Vatican City, bisecting a courtyard originally designed by Bramante.

top of a hill in Trastevere, and it gave me the flexibility to move around quickly. All of the residents would eat together, since a major intention of the Academy is to connect people, share thoughts, and have discussions. I also met many people from similar institutions in Rome.

At one dinner in particular, I was sitting next to a scholar specializing in books from the Middle Ages—89 years young, a very smart woman named Peggy Brown—who was curious about my work after I told her that I was a book designer. I brought her to my studio, where I had organized a kind of exhibition of the *many* books I brought with me, and when she saw my work, she saw a connection to her work and the books in the Vatican Library. Peggy told me that I urgently needed to go there. She went there every day herself to research something very specific. I never believed that I would be allowed in, since the library is only for scholars, but she told me, "Write a letter. Explain what you want to study. At least try it." I wrote a letter with my intentions, had it translated into Italian, went in for an interview, and was given permission.

As it turned out, there was interest at the BAV in my desire to research the book from a bookmaker's perspective. I studied the book as a whole. I almost worked as a codicologist. I was, and still am, studying the book itself: the size, weight, material, text structure, title, contents, and so on. I wanted to discover what happened to the book over time because I think books are more limited than ever before. I wanted to figure out why that happened.

During my time at the American Academy, I was invited to give a lecture at the Dutch equivalent of the Academy, the Royal Netherlands Institute Rome. They were so intrigued by the subject matter that they encouraged me to continue my research and gave me a three-and-a-half-month residency. I was the only nonacademic in the institute, and it was super interesting to discuss my thoughts and ideas with scientists.

KH   The collection of the Vatican Library is so vast though. It holds centuries of manuscripts and books in different languages and from different civilizations. How do you approach such a formidable amount of material and find what relates to you?

IB   I had to set my own rules to find the books I was looking for. Professor Jeroen Jansen, a Dutch book historian from the University of Amsterdam was a very good adviser and supporter. He knows the library well and gave me very good suggestions. The Vatican librarians were, of course, also essential to navigating the collection.

It was and continues to be an interesting experience for me! I found books which relate to my own work. I am criticized a lot for not following the rules in my book designs, and so it was a nice discovery that my work shares connections with some of the books in the BAV.

The *SHV Think Book*, a 2136-page book, was published in 1996. It has no page numbers, no paragraph breaks, none of the conventions we hold today really. It was often described as an avant-garde book, but it became clear to me it is not at all avant-garde. I found out that early books had the same structure as the *SHV Think Book*—but hundreds of years earlier. I realized that whatever I am doing in my own work now, and maybe this applies to making in general, has already been done before.

Why did we develop the elements of book design in such conventional ways then? The book is not only a container of thought but has transformed to serve as a marketing tool as well. When early books were made, nobody thought about the book cover. They thought about the spine so that a book could be found on the bookshelf.

KH   The spine is what you saw.

IB   Yes, it's the spine that is important to the book owner and to libraries. People recognize the book by the spine, but in the bookstore, the cover is most visible! I looked at these elements from the maker's perspective and then investigated why they may have changed over time.

I realized that there are reasons for the way I intuitively play with all of these elements, and I began to find these reasons in the library. It has been an enormous revelation. In the end, I spent six months at the BAV. I wanted to go back last year as well but couldn't because of COVID. Now I have a few weeks rescheduled, and I will continue to return until I make a publication.

KH   What kind of publication? Will you do your own *Elements of Architecture*, but *Elements of Bookmaking*, perhaps?

IB   In a way, *Elements of Bookmaking* is a very good idea, which I investigate, of course, but the more precise topic is *What Happened to the Book*. That is the working title and the core of what I'm looking into. Bookmaking is more conservative than ever because of the enormous dominance of marketing. It has become all about selling, but I think in order to sell, it's not about compromising the content and design but making

89

a good book. You won't sell books because of a commercial cover. If it's good, it will work.

KH   And people will be interested.

IB   Exactly. The Sheila Hicks book is my manifesto for the book. I was fired by the New York commissioner on that job. Nobody believed that it would ever be a success. I proposed a subtle cover, a graphic interpretation of Sheila's work embossed on the front. It is a completely white book with a cover that is barely visible and the publisher said, "Nobody will be able to see this cover on the internet. We won't sell it and we will go bankrupt." All of these negative things were said and assumed.

Of course, the book was published the way I envisioned it. I am very stubborn. It is not because I am convinced that what I am doing is good but because I am curious to see the book made. The moment you have the book in your hands, you can touch it and experience it, and you do not want to put it down. In the end, it became one of the most successful books I have ever made. It's going into the sixth printing already.

KH   It would be a shame for design decisions to be directed by the need to be noticed online. The possibility of seeing nothing more than a blank page online is something that I really enjoy about the cover for the Sheila Hicks book, actually. I appreciate the quiet but forceful way it demands focus on the texture and shadow of the book even in its digital presence. The book you made for Chanel is also exceptional in this same way. It has an incredible tactile experience with a nearly absent digital presence.

IB   It's good that you mention this. The Chanel book could never function digitally or as a PDF—there would be nothing to see. It is a book that only works as an analog object. I wanted to create something almost nonexistent yet very present like the content of the book, the history of Chanel No. 5. Thinking of books online: do you know that you can study many of the Vatican's books digitally?

KH   Yes, I've really enjoyed browsing through their digital collection.

IB   The website is great, but to study the physical book, which is the essence of what I do, to feel the weight and understand the dimensions, it is crucial to be in the library. The book is a cultural object and making books is a cultural action, like

A table of six small scenes summarize Virgil's allusions to familiar Greek mythology in the introductory section of Book 3 of the *Georgics*. He aims to surpass Greek pastoral poetry with his own poetry. Vat. lat. 3225. © 2021 Biblioteca Apostolica Vaticana.

SEDNONNULLAMACISVIRESINDUSTRIAFIRMAT
QUAMVENEREMETCAECISTIMULOSAVERTEREAMORIS
SIVEBOVOMSIVEESTQUOGRATIORUSUSEQUORUM
ATQUEIDEOTAUROSPROCULATQUEINSOLARELIGANT
PASCUALOSTAMONTEMOPPOSITUMETTRANSFLUMINAIXTA
ALTERATITICCINICOSSATURAAASPRAESEPIASERVANT

Two bulls fight over a desired cow. The defeated bull exercises in preparation to resume battle in the future. This scene occurs within a section on animal husbandry. Vat. lat. 3225. © 2021 Biblioteca Apostolica Vaticana.

IRMA BOOM WITH KIMBERLEY HUGGINS

The Digital Vatican Library was launched in 2010, following a long period of renovation and modernization. It is an effort to fulfill the higher ideals of the library, to both preserve and share knowledge, while also practically overcoming an ineffective catalogue system. As recently as 1993, two-thirds of the Vatican's holdings had not been cataloged. To find a document, you needed to first find someone who knew where to find it.

making paintings, for example. It should not be questioned whether books should still be made, but I get that question a lot: "Why are you still making books?" The printed book is a fundamental and integral part of our tradition and culture, of published and public knowledge and wisdom. My research at the Vatican made me realize even more how relevant making books is for our shared memory and history. The flux inherent to the internet doesn't allow you to have that kind of reflection. A book is one of the most stable media!

Whatever is written in the book remains there. Therefore, you don't make libraries and books for the present or for the past, you make them as a reference vehicle for the future.

KH   I read once that you described books, similarly to how you are describing them now, as tools to freeze a moment. That description stuck with me, books as edited compilations of memory.

IB   Books capture a moment, which is crucial. I teach and give workshops, and when I give assignments to make a book, I often have to convince students of the value of doing so. Young people who are engaged with social media consider the book outdated. I have to come prepared with good arguments that support why the book has to be made. I tell them, "This is a chance to really think about what is important in your life right now and to document it in such a way that you can return to it your whole life." The moment you leave university and enter into the professional life is a crucial one. This is a moment when you don't have any commissions, there are no assignments, nothing but your own thoughts. To freeze that moment, I think is crucial in everyone's life.

KH   So, the making of a book can preserve a version of you in your lifetime?

IB   Absolutely. The library is a reference for humanity, but books can also be a reference for your own universe. Maybe I am giving the book too high a podium, but I really think that books are effective vehicles to share information with others *and* yourself. To make and to edit that single thing brings all your loose ends, all your thoughts together. It is analogous to the work of an orchestra conductor or even a film director. You have to assemble elements together into something unified to make a composition, to make a film, or to make a book.

93

KH   I like thinking about bookmaking this way, that deliberately documenting your world can help keep you centered through all the changes of a career. Throughout your own career, you have remained steadfast in your belief in your designs even in the face of controversy. How do you find courage to remain committed to your instincts?

IB   I must say, I also think of that in respect to myself—how did I dare to do it? It's strange actually. With the Sheila Hicks book, for example, Sheila called me and I immediately envisioned this book. I envisioned the book immediately in my mind, but if something exists only in your mind, it doesn't exist. It has to be materialized. I do everything to make that specific book that I have in my mind. It has to be precisely this thing, and it took maybe 50 or so models to get close to executing the vision properly. What you see in your head is often nicer and better than the reality of making, but the effort is put toward coming as close as possible to the concept.

    I will make the book even when nobody wants it anymore. This obsessiveness ends up being entirely internal because, for me, communicating my process can be difficult. It is in my head, and sometimes I cannot express it immediately as a model, as an object only exists when it's executed, when it's printed on a press, when it's bound, and when it's in your hands. That is my only proof. I always have to make a model by hand to realize ideas and make it better. It has to be made seriously and precisely.

KH   Did you discover historical techniques while at the Vatican that you hope to implement in ongoing projects?

IB   Yes, but what I thought was more interesting actually was the way the research resolved my thinking about past projects. For instance, I used this specific edge for the Sheila Hicks book. It gives this special experience to the book. Sheila Hicks once said to me, "It looks like the dog has bitten the edges." I often experiment with things that are not done, and I have a lot of stamina to make things happen! People think that these ideas are crazy but I found these soft edges in old books—they were the result of a knife having been used to open the book.

    I get a lot of inspiration studying books at the Vatican, but for me, there's also a peace of mind. It totally changed my life. There really is a before-the-Vatican and an after-the-Vatican. I am totally addicted to studying books.

94

FORSITANETPINGUISHORTOSQUAEICURACOLENDI
ORNARETCANEREMBITERIQUEROSARINDISTI
QUOQ·MODOPOTISGAUDERENTINTIBARIUIS
ETUIRIDISAPPIORIEAFIORTUSQUEFERHERBAM
CRESCERETINUENTREMCUCUMISNECSERACOMANTI
NARCISSUMAUTFLEXITACUSSTUIMINACANTHI
PALLENTISHEDERASETAMANTISLITORAMYRTOS

An old man from Corycus who lives on a few acres of wasteland explains the delight he finds in his garden and the honey his bees provide. The last book of the *Georgics* is devoted to beekeeping. Vat. lat. 3225. © 2021 Biblioteca Apostolica Vaticana.

KH   Would you share a book that was especially exciting for you to study?

IB   You know that I work with Rem Koolhaas, right? We have done a seemingly endless number of competition books for OMA but also published books like *Project Japan*, *Elements of Architecture* and the Guggenheim book, *Countryside, A Report*. While I was at the Vatican, I was also working on the *Countryside* project with him.

KH   Quick aside, but I just want to point out that the book you made for *Countryside, The Future* ended up being the only way many people could experience that exhibition.

IB   Can you imagine! Rem worked for six years on that exhibition, I worked on it for about two years, and then after three weeks the exhibition closed! It was such an anticlimax. Unbelievable. But indeed, my contributions to the *Countryside* project were affected by my presence at the Vatican.

The oldest book in the Vatican Library is an illuminated manuscript of poems by Virgil dated to roughly 400 AD. It is an amazing book, one of the most modern that I've seen in the Vatican. It is a square book with a beautiful, almost modern script and beautiful illustrations. I could see the facsimile version of it. I have seen an original sheet of the book when it was exhibited very briefly on a special occasion. It is extremely fragile. I was so excited, I still have the text messages that I sent Rem to share my excitement. This is why one of the illustrations was placed at the very beginning of the exhibition.

I continued searching though because, while I love manuscripts, I am totally fascinated by books after Gutenberg, the incunabula. My pure interest lies in the book as a printed entity where the print run is not a few copies but significant.

At some point, I began researching book sizes at the Vatican. Early books were sometimes intentionally small so that they could be put in a pocket, but these books came before Gutenberg. I was looking for the first printed pocketbook. After Gutenberg, books became more democratic and more copies were available. The first printed and published pocketbook was made in 1501 by Aldus Manutius in Venice. It's an incredible and beautiful book, but I realized, "Oh my god, it's also the Virgil!" It was the poem, the laudation of the countryside again! It was typeset in italics and printed as the first pocketbook.

The Aldine Virgil was the first in a series that Aldus Manutius (1455-1515) printed in the octavo format, a smaller and portable format previously used for devotional books. By applying it to secular texts, the concept of reading for personal pleasure began to develop.

IRMA BOOM WITH KIMBERLEY HUGGINS

I was so excited. I decided that the dimensions of the Guggenheim's *Countryside* book should replicate those of the Manutius pocketbook. Back in the Netherlands, I made models of the size, and Rem fell immediately in love with it. Eventually the book became a bestseller, in part because the exhibition closed, and the book began to act as the ambassador for the exhibition. That is what excites me because that is what a book should be, something that goes into the world.

KH   It reveals something special, to consider yourself tied to this specific thread of books and their makers, stretching all the way from the 4th century to 1501 to now.

IB   And there are actually details from a number of Vatican books that I applied in my own work. For example, paper was costly, so it was used in an efficient way. I also found these empty spots in the text, presumably reserved to add Greek text. I used these empty spots in a different way, to start new paragraphs.

We even tried to mimic an old typeface to recreate this specific atmosphere you find in old books. We drew the typeface with a Bic pen, which Rem Koolhaas always uses.

KH   What if we looked at the personal library that you have been building with the funding from the Johannes Vermeer Award? How do you evaluate potential books for your own library?

IB   What I am collecting are books from the 1960s, 1500s, and 1600s. Books from these periods demonstrate freedom and creativity in the use of materials, typography, sizes of the books, and structure of the texts. It has been an enormous source of inspiration. I have about 150 books now.

These are two moments in bookmaking when it was free and new. After Gutenberg, there were no conventions in place, and so the incunabula of this time period were very free and interesting books. The further you go into the 16th, 17th, 18th, 19th centuries, the more conventional the book becomes, the higher the print run, the more standardization. But then in the '60s, after the war, there was this crazy moment where bookmaking was suddenly free again. The world changed so much and so did the attitude toward the book. If you place books from these two moments together, if I put *Turkish Delight* from 1969 next to an incunabula for example, then you will see a relationship and you will see that they work together.

This is why the incunabula are an enormous source of inspiration, especially for typography.

in·cu·na·bu·la
/ in-kyə-ˈna-byə-lə /

plural noun
1. Latin for "in the cradle", is a title given to the earliest printed books, generally prior to 1501, when the printing process was still in its infancy.

The Vatican holds a collection of 8,000 incunabula.

KH It is a common dilemma in design, whether to abide by conventions or break them freely. How do you encourage people to remain open to remixing their field for themselves? Do you have advice?

IB Keep going and keep making, that is what I teach. As a result, you can develop quickly. Whether the final thing is a book or an object, you develop much faster through the act of making and the production. Don't be scared, you'll learn the most from the failures.

KH This brings to mind your lecture at the GSD, where you spoke about your experiences with doubt as a young designer and how your view of doubt changed from a fault to an advantage in "a quest for perfection." Do you still have moments of self-doubt?

IB I am a doubter. I will keep checking out new perspectives right until the deadline—or even after the deadline!

The doubt tells you that you're thinking. If you don't have doubt, then you're certain of what to do, and you just go do it. Doubting is important. It gives you moments to reconsider. If there was no deadline, I would not stop making changes until the very last minute. The deadline helps me to make decisions.

Still, I always wonder, when do they find out that I'm not good enough? When do people unveil me? That's why my personal book is so small: because I still have a lot to learn and have to become better. The book grows every year, by three percent, and in the end, when I'm 80, I'll have a book of a large size. It grows with the idea that to become better, you keep practicing. It's an ongoing process of learning and trying to get somewhere. That's what keeps me going. I'm curious about what's next.

98

Kathryn Yusoff

with Maxwell Smith-Holmes

Images Not Available

On Race, the Underground, and the Museum

MAXWELL SMITH-HOLMES   For some time now, your work has been influential in the design disciplines, particularly in landscape architecture, and you recently lectured at the GSD. I'm curious if you have any reflections on how designers receive your research. I ask because architects and landscape architects have always been interested in geology, which your work implicates in structures of racialized violence in a way that complicates the built environment.

KATHRYN YUSOFF   I think in some ways it's interesting that geography and design don't have more conversations. I feel like I'm just beginning to get into conversations with architects, even though I trained as a designer. There are a lot of shared concerns around thinking about materiality and, particularly in the context of the Anthropocene, what we might think of as urban strata and their impact in terms of extraction and climate change. I'm detecting a moment in architecture where there's this shift away from the object and the built environment, and, for me, the flip side of that movement is thinking about the absences that make a building. The urban burrows deep into the earth.

Some of the historical work that I've been doing on geology, which I talked about in the lecture, is around industrialization and how, when you float materials such as steel on the stock market and into the sky, it requires racialized undergrounds to materialize that value, and these are always absent from the articulation of that materiality. I think we're at this moment where there is a turn toward the elemental as some form of a new ontology that, to me, is very problematic. Material economies, metallurgy, and minerals are all caught up with geologies of race not just in production but in the very transformation of the earth as an earth through colonialism. So, this raises questions about the type of planetarity that is being imagined and about how we engage now with the coupling of a fast-shifting geologic time and racial justice.

101

Screenshot from the Peabody Museum of Archaeology and Ethnography online collections database, accessed October 30, 2020. Courtesy of Kathryn Yusoff.

MS   The Peabody Museum of Archaeology and Ethnography at Harvard has a searchable online database of the institution's collections, which include photographs from Louis Agassiz's 19th-century expeditions to South America and Africa that document Black and Indigenous individuals as ethnographic subjects. Much of this archival material has not been digitized, so some of Agassiz's photographs are available online as only a thumbnail of text reading "Image not Available." In these withheld images, do you see a dynamic between racialized undergrounds and surface, i.e., between rare-earth minerals or other extracted geological materials and the graphical user interface?

KY   I think the primary concern for me is thinking about the transposition of whiteness as both a material economy and an affectual economy, what I call an "affective infrastructure": the metaphor and materiality of whiteness always levitates off the Black and brown undergrounds.[1] The "Image not Available" brings this tension to the fore by pointing to the way in which

1   Kathryn Yusoff, "Epochal Aesthetics: Affectual Infra-structures of the Anthropocene," *e-flux architecture*, March 29, 2017, https://www.e-flux.com/architecture/accumulation/121847/epochal-aesthetics-affectual-infrastructures-of-the-anthropocene/.

KATHRYN YUSOFF WITH MAXWELL SMITH-HOLMES

Screenshot from the Peabody Museum of Archaeology and Ethnography online collections database, accessed September 2, 2021. Courtesy of Maxwell Smith-Holmes.

the history of extraction (material and psychic) persists in the present as the empirical bedrock of knowledge in the university and as the basis of its expertise and legacy. Those images from Louis Agassiz's Brazil expedition, while not as well-known or contested as his images made of enslaved persons, are part of the visual dismemberment of race produced by geologists at that particular moment in the late 18th and early 19th centuries. Although race is obviously not a scientifically valid concept, there's a question here about what *allows* race to act as if it were a real thing. I've been interested in the metaepistemological foundation of how race is made as a conceptual and material force: How is race made through the governance of "geopower," and, how is it made through sedimentations of aesthetic-empirical objects that organize subjectivity in ways that stratify the idea of the human? What are the similarities between the organization of identity in

IMAGES NOT AVAILABLE

terms of personhood and the organization of materiality in terms of natural resources? How do the inhuman and inhumane go together as a paradigm of extraction?

We see the "Image not Available" on the screen being materialized through the rare-earth minerals that comprise electronics and are mined by the racialized poor; this parallels the same formations of racial undergrounds as those that were being constructed by Agassiz when the images were made. These images were made in 1865 on an expedition to Brazil that Agassiz went on with a number of other geologists and the philosopher William James under the patronage of the monarch Don Pedro II. Agassiz had over 400 photographs commissioned, mostly of partially undressed or fully undressed Indigenous and Black women and men. The "Image not Available" is on the cusp of acknowledging that visual dismemberment while not reproducing it for consumption. But this is also a past that is not fully acknowledged in the sense of the full history of those images in the present. The Agassiz legacy at Harvard is in the process of being addressed, but it still remains very much sedimented into the institution and in much broader knowledge economies and metaepistemologies of the humanities and science.[2]

2 Juliet E. Isselbacher, "Agassiz Name on Harvard Campus Honors Not Louis Agassiz, But Wife and Son," in *The Crimson*, April 4, 2019, https://www.thecrimson.com/article/2019/4/4/agassiz-name-and-legacy/.

MS   In your talk, you said that the university is not so different from the prison mine.

KY   Yes, these are institutions that are historically in conversation! In the US, geology becomes this populist science because it is the praxis of "settlement." Enslavers think of themselves as geologists and need geologic surveying to develop land. They also think about themselves as located in geologies of race and see themselves as involved in "managing" racial populations. Geology and race go hand in hand throughout US history, as in most settler-colonial societies, especially with the Homestead Act's domestication of forms of geologic management of land. I think it's really important to think about a figure like Agassiz as a populist figure: he's in a position of extreme power at Harvard, he's writing letters to politicians, he's advising the Freedmen's Inquiry Commission after Reconstruction, and he's lecturing down in South Carolina to enslavers about white supremacy as a geologic fact.

Agassiz founded the first natural history museum in the US, Harvard's Museum of Comparative Zoology, which set the classification standards for natural history museums in this country. It set out how to catalog species and

KATHRYN YUSOFF WITH MAXWELL SMITH-HOLMES

how to produce scientific subjects. These institutions do more than just hold knowledge. They talk to and engage with other sites of extraction for an episteme of racial production. For me, making these kinds of interdisciplinary connections is really important for thinking about the politics of our institutions today and how we think about colonization and anti-racist practices within the university. This is not just about addressing the racial ideas of particular figures but about understanding how race is fundamental to the material development of settler colonialism and its ideas about what materiality is. Ideas of the telos of race and the telos of materiality through the development of natural resources are held together through the very foundation of the nation. Agassiz was in Brazil making visual maps of rivers and making visual lexicons of race. His expressed concern was to show the failure of the Brazilian race "experiment" as a warning to the South (and North) of the dangers of racial mixing or miscegenation. His wife, who was the co-founder and first president of the Radcliffe Institute for Advanced Study, assisted in cajoling women to undress so that he could photograph them as primitive and degenerate.

MS   What would it mean if the images were made publicly available in the online archive? How do various cataloging practices and degrees of public accessibility function along a spectrum ranging from, at one end, exacerbating racialized visual dismemberment to, at the opposite end, addressing the histories of racist thought embedded in institutions like the university?

KY   Many Black feminist scholars have argued that this kind of reproduction can also be a way of furthering that initial violence and continuing to add to an affectual architecture of the availability of Black and brown women's bodies for violent consumption. I want to think very carefully about how you intervene in forms of reproducing violence, thinking with the work of Saidiya Hartman, Hazel Carby, and Christina Sharpe, to name a few thinkers on care in the archive. The question is how do you intervene in the architectures of violence and form resistances within that material. The descendants of the photographs of the enslaved have made some suggestions. You can point the finger or throw a rock at Agassiz and say he's a racist scientist, but in some ways that misses the point of the effect of the combined sciences and political seeing that produce this idea of racial difference, which is really difficult to get away from because it has structured so much of the geo-logics of development and the material experience of race. The persistence of the affective architectures of the idea of race is as powerful as the material force of it.

MS   Do you have any advice for architects, landscape architects, and urban planners—who do work every day rearranging mineral matter—on how their work might hold some sort of radical potential?

KY   If you think about everything that's taken away to build something—the *unarchitectural*—and you think about all those absent and racialized undergrounds, how can they become present within the very space that erases them? Often the architectural brief is to not make them present, right? During the January 6th attack on the Capitol, for example, I was thinking about the Alabama marble that's on the Lincoln Memorial and inside the Senate, which was most likely mined by leased incarcerated laborers. Young Black boys and men that had their futures stolen and were placed in prison mines. I was thinking about the relationship between embodiment and geology, how a building can embody its mineral histories in not just the nice kind of fossil surfaces of various bygone epochs but in *who* and *what* has touched a material in its surfacing. The Martinican poet and political activist Aimé Césaire talked about the heel print of the enslaved on every skyscraper. What do these ghost geologies leave behind? What are the portals that can be mobilized to tell these erased histories and bring the flesh of geology into a reckoning with the present and its racial inequalities?

     I just started working on a project with my colleagues Casper Laing Ebbensgaard and Kerry Holden that looks at "planetary portals" for the architecture humanities conference that the Pratt Institute is organizing in 2022. The plan is to do some quarrying on Governors Island, because all the soil from the subway that was cleared by African American laborers went to Governors Island. We're thinking about the soil as part of the architecture of cultural memory—not in a forensic way but as a material medium for doing temporal reclamation work. We are also looking at Cecil Rhodes as an infrastructural portal and examining the way he went from a slumlord in East London to the uberimperialist of Africa and how his legacy might be contested despite much of his infrastructural organization of race and matter remaining intact. In the work of Forensic Architecture and others, I think there's a promissory quality about visually revealing something. I go in a slightly different direction: the aesthetics of race is already so much a part of our forms of spatial and material language that you have to address it in an aesthetic register that does not reinstate the grammars of geology that segregate forms of knowledge and their embodied racial geologies—because that's exactly what people like Louis Agassiz were doing. Conversations around respatializing those sets of interdisciplinary relationships between race and affect as an *architecture* are crucial to have between geographers and architects. Architects have a material mode of work and an attention to spatial practice but might be trained to think about materiality through an elemental lens. I think we are at the beginning of seeing just what that dialogue can look like and what it might mean to mobilize that anti-colonial will *materially* as an anti-racist spatial occupation.

MS   Yes, I think that designers have a very grounded relationship to materiality, but it can be a way of looking at materials that erases how they came into being.

KY   Yes. Architectural surfaces materialize through forms of erasure and extraction. One of the things that the Anthropocene brings into play is how architectures of time are mapped into building through materiality as urban strata and at a granular level. Those processes of materialization also come into being through the time of the subjects. A lot of architectural discourse is about futurity, looking toward a speculative horizon rather than looking at what constructs that horizon! I think we are beginning to see a shift in architectural discourse toward undergrounds that feed the surface of the built environment, and I would insist that these are always racialized undergrounds, material hierarchies of racialized relations that govern the possibilities of space and its production.

109

Jorge Silvetti

with Nicolás Delgado Álcega

Labyrinth of Affinities

On Perspective, Anamorphosis, and Repositionings

K. Michael Hays, *Unprecedented Realism: The Architecture of Machado and Silvetti.* Princeton, NJ: Princeton Architectural Press, 1995.

The following conversation developed through a periodic set of exchanges that took place between September 2020 and March 2021. As a series of social events unfolded—at the GSD, in the United States, and around the world—the authors opened up a discussion that began with a set of personal notes that Jorge Silvetti had collected in the months prior. Alarming current events catalyzed a slow discussion, one in which personal experiences, disciplinary issues, and large cultural processes constantly intertwined through an exchange of words and images; one through which the authors, both raised surrounded by a degree of social unrest, sought to make sense of what they saw around them.

This conversation took place amidst Silvetti's retirement from the GSD after 46 years of involvement in the school. It accompanied the donation process of the Machado & Silvetti archive to the Frances Loeb Library and paralleled a seminar at the GSD in which related issues were engaged through a different mode. It precedes a retrospective exhibition of the work of Machado & Silvetti and has been a sounding board for a new course that Silvetti will teach as a research professor in the coming years. It is a conversation between two South Americans from opposite ends of the continent and on opposite ends of their professional careers, who are both curious, concerned, and stimulated by this moment in the history of architectural culture.

Rodolfo Machado, Jorge Silvetti, Peter G. Rowe, and Gabriel Feld. *Rodolfo Machado and Jorge Silvetti : Buildings for Cities.* Cambridge, MA: Harvard University Graduate School of Design, 1989.

Javier Cenicacelaya, Íñigo Saloña, and Nader Tehrani. *The Work of Machado & Silvetti = La Obra de Machado & Silvetti.* San Francisco Bay Area: Oro Editions, 2018.

NICOLÁS DELGADO ÁLCEGA   In preparation for our conversation, I have been going over your office's three monographs, because I wanted to have a discussion with you about your long-standing interest in the history of architecture. To that end, the projects in the monographs that you and Rodolfo produced in Sicily over the years struck me as a good place to start.

How did you get to Sicily? And why did it capture your professional and intellectual attention for so many years?

PAIRS

JORGE SILVETTI   Before I answer your question, let me first say that I was chiefly educated within the context of the Western tradition but from a distinctly *marginal location*. I was raised in Buenos Aires, a city at the bottom of the Western world, in the southernmost tip of the continent. At the 34th parallel south, I was not only literally at the geographic bottom of the world but also on the fringes of the history of Western society. When I say marginal then, I mean simply that I was in a position at an edge farthest away from the centers of cultural dominance.

From Buenos Aires everything was far, particularly those centers of power and their histories. This was amplified by the fact that, back then, people didn't travel that often to Europe. To do so affordably meant a month-long journey by boat, and even that option was not available to middle-class families.

Nonetheless, everything I was learning in school—music, history, art—was invariably founded on the Western tradition. It was assumed that everything you were learning was the way it was supposed to be, which I suppose today means "canonical." But I grew up feeling that whatever my reality was, it was upended from that "normality." So, my understanding of the canonical was always inevitably skewed by the particular angle from where I had been positioned by fate, where distant traditions were intertwined with other local cultural ingredients that fed my mind and imagination. In marginal positions, local cultural pressures are inescapably very active. This is particularly true in the arts, language, and daily customs, whether it's classical or pop music, painting, literature, cuisine, or local jargon.

All these elements that were bound by location coalesced into my individual cultural profile. They contaminated my understanding and regard for the "canon"—my way of *seeing* it—and importantly influenced and inspired my creative and intellectual work. I think this all points to my particular, seemingly deviant predilections and interests among the canonical expressions of Western architecture, which are generally found in places that are far from the accepted "center," be it Athens, Rome, or Paris. Even though the Hagia Sophia or El Escorial were presented as part of the canon, I was always inclined to interpret them as marginal. I found them to be anomalies, deviations, or even perversions by which I was fascinated.

However, these conditions not only determined my interest in certain cases on the edge of the canon, they also influenced my reading of works squarely in line with the canon.

po·si·tion
/ pəˈziSH(ə)n /

noun
1. a place where something is located
2. a particular way in which something is placed or arranged
3. a situation or set of circumstances that affect one's power to act
4. a person's point of view or attitude toward something

verb
1. put or arrange something in a particular place or way
2. promote a product
3. portray or regard someone as a particular type of person

re·gard
/ rəˈgärd /

noun
1. attention to
2. best wishes

verb
1. consider (something) in a specified way
2. gaze at steadily in a specified fashion

112

At one point, I even convinced myself that the whole Palladian oeuvre was a peculiar, provincial oddity of the Roman Renaissance. Although I used to be somewhat embarrassed of myself for holding these positions—keeping most to myself—today I am convinced that we can and should present Palladio's work first and foremost as such. Certainly at least the corpus of his domestic architecture around Vicenza! Those sober, restrained, stuccoed villas qua farms screaming their classical pedigree yet speaking a "dialect" far from Rome and Florence, to which they allude. I think today they become clearer and more powerful when seen this way. It makes them more productive and meaningful in the context of our current concerns. Ultimately, it shows convincingly that the canon is an ever changing, layered, and shifting body of models and ideals. Seen this way, Palladio's work moves quickly from being marginal to becoming central to the canon, not only in Italy but all over Europe and eventually North America.

This way of seeing is, really, the indelible mark that this "position"—physical, historical, cultural—left on my persona and the perspective from which I look at the world. And today it explains to me—even if it's too late for my mother of Tuscan origins to understand!—why I became so enchanted and involved with Sicilian architecture and its intensely hybrid and exuberant artistic pedigree.

per·spec·tive
/ pər'spektiv /

noun
1. the art of drawing solid objects on a two-dimensional surface so as to give the correct impression of their height, width, depth, and position in relation to each other when viewed from za particular point
2. particular attitude toward or way of regarding something; a point of view
3. gaze at steadily in a specified fashion

NDA   You're suggesting Sicily has a similar condition to that of Buenos Aires? Of being at the edge of a culturally dominant center that it is in contact with?

JS   In some ways, say in relation to Rome, Florence, or Venice during classical periods, yes. Sicily is a place where this phenomenon is very much a part of the island's cultural condition and history. When viewed from the position of dominant cultural centers, it is a culture that has been marginal to other centralities for millennia: to the Phoenicians, the ancient Greeks, the Romans, the Byzantines, the Normans, the Spanish, and so on.

So, Sicily is a place where all major cultures converged, but for which Sicily was never a particular center. And yet, when you see things *from* Sicily, the island prompts its own form of centrality. This duality is inevitable in Sicily. On a map, we can see it as an ineludible roadblock in the *Mare Nostrum* upon which all Mediterranean cultures stumbled and "accidentally" left their marks. But conversely, we can also see it as a "center" of Mediterranean culture, which collected the tolls

anamorphic
/ˌanəˈmôrfik /

adjective
1. denoting or relating to projection or drawing distorted by anamorphosis

paid by all the passersby that helped create and enrich its own particular cultural makeup. The deep layers of cultural stratification caused by this geographical, cultural condition have produced something unique in Sicily that is still palpable today.

Nowhere is this clearer than in Sicilian Baroque architecture, a local strain of what was otherwise a Roman cultural epiphenomenon. In Sicily, the Roman Baroque is appropriated and completely reinvented. Its exaggeration, ebullience, and luxuriance goes far beyond Rome's, and its urban ambition is much more comprehensively realized. The architectural and urban planning experiments of the Val di Noto, as well as the codevelopment of sculpture, ornament, and stucco in Palermo have few parallels elsewhere during this time.

The same can be said of the so-called "Norman architecture," a short period in the late 11th and most of the 12th century, where an original architecture was created by the fusion and coalescence of Byzantine, Islamic, and Norman architectural streams.

NDA   For how long were you actually involved with research and projects in Sicily?

JS   It was about 11 years. We would spend every moment we didn't have to be in Boston in Sicily. And when we were in Boston, there was usually ongoing work for Sicily at the office. It was undoubtedly one of the most formative experiences of my life, professionally and intellectually. I don't think I learned more about architecture in any other place. Sicily is a place where I understood so much about how cultures are put in motion and transformed.

NDA   In a way, your journeys to Sicily sound like the more canonical pilgrimage to Rome, but instead of offering the "definitive" references of antiquity or the Baroque, Sicily offered uniquely "derivative" ones.

JS   Well, firstly I would never call what Sicily produced a "derivative" type of work, which has a derogatory connotation. This is architecture that I would call original, fresh, and powerful. As to your other point about an alternative canonical pilgrimage, I'm not so sure about that. I knew Rome well before I went to work in Sicily. However, by the time I got to the American Academy in 1986, I had been involved in Sicily for four or five years. So at that point, it was in fact Sicily that tainted a posteriori my mature understanding of the Rome I thought I knew well and not the other way around.

114

NDA We normally judge what is "on the edge" by contrasting it with what is at the center, with the canonical reference. I think this idea of reading things the other way around, as you are describing, is interesting. Looking back at the reference or origin point from what you've learned at the edge.

I guess if you think about it, it's the only way. We are always seeing from our point of view, with all of the baggage that this implies.

JS Absolutely. This is actually at the core of what the so-called "Western tradition" truly is, or at least, that is how I have come to understand it. I think this is the way we should always position ourselves to look at any cultural practice.

Now that I have been relieved of most of my academic responsibilities, I've been working on a seminar that tries to reframe what we understand by the Western tradition and leaves behind this notion of "canon," which I don't believe is really a solid, homogeneous, and compact cultural phenomenon. It is an attempt to reposition my thinking around the topics that have occupied my mind as a teacher and practitioner, which has been fueled and energized with great impetus in the past year, since we have all felt the need to move at a different pace with sharper focus and new objectives.

My main intent is to dismantle the idea that the Western tradition is a monolithic, static, and intrinsically problematic thing, as it has become customary to describe it. While this is not a particularly original idea—scholars like Salvatore Settis have dealt with this idea in great depth already—I think we have much to gain by restating this fact. I believe we should try to further understand the ways in which this tradition is an ever changing, highly heterogeneous, macrocultural formation that has been around for thousands of years. The Western tradition is a cultural phenomenon that has had quite a few dominant strains at different times and has always been fueled, energized, and transformed by the internal dynamics of its intrinsic diversity, by the interplay of its component parts.

What I hope to achieve with the course is to take this tradition and see how once "marginal" or "dominated" component strains of its diversity have at times advanced to become dominant themselves—Palladio, again … For me, cases of this kind are evidence that the attempts we are undertaking to respond to today's issues require—or better, deserve—reconsideration. I think that by repositioning our strategic intellectual perspective in order to productively work from within this collective of cultural strains—instead of taking

re·po·si·tion
/ ˌrēpəˈziSHən /

verb
1. place in a different position
2. adjust or alter the position of

on an approach of rejection—our capacity to amplify certain strains is much higher.

I'm actually of the opinion that going as far back as the Acropolis of Athens—two and a half millennia behind us—gives us incredible opportunities to study strains that deal with issues that are at the forefront of our concern right now, whether related to identity, diversity, inclusion, or justice. In fact, the course may be called "The Acropolis of Athens and Its Consequences."

NDA It's exciting to think that architecture can play a role in these changing balances of power. But can it actually operate at the speed necessary for it to be proactive in these processes?

JS I think we have to understand architecture as part of the constellation of cultural products that define a moment. In academia, we lately tend to fall under the temptation of making architecture overreach into other domains of society and culture in which other practices are more effective and powerful. But if we look at cases in a nuanced way, I believe we can see many of these forces at play in the making of architecture.

A lot of the interests I will be exploring in the seminar began developing years ago in some option studios I taught at the GSD. In the courses, we would deal directly with the profound and tense issues of cultural identity and diversity that characterize our age through many cases, including, for instance, the Indigenous Guaraní cultural territory, a place that exists at the intersection of several South American nation-states.

We took as a starting point the physical remains of the *Misiones jesuíticas*: a century-and-a-half-long colonial cultural project that spanned the 17th and 18th centuries. The *misiones* were the result of interactions between European architectural culture and local practices. The combination of these two traditions under the extreme environmental conditions of this area produced a form of heritage that differed greatly from the better-known, typical outcomes of the Spanish colonial sociopolitical models prevalent at the time.

There was clearly at play here a power dynamic in which one of the parties was still under the control of another. And yet, the remains of the architecture that we still see there are the result of an act of cultural negotiation, one which had ultimately produced something altogether new, distinct, and extraordinary from either perspective. The architecture did not vindicate any specific individual or wholeheartedly upend

"There are those who want a text (an art, a painting) without a shadow, without the 'dominant ideology'; but this is to want a text without fecundity, without productivity, a sterile text ... The text needs its shadows; this shadow is a bit of ideology, a bit of representation, a bit of subject: ghosts, pockets, traces, necessary clouds: subversion must produce its own chiaroscuro." —Roland Barthes, *The Pleasure of the Text*, 1975.

JORGE SILVETTI WITH NICOLÁS DELGADO ÁLCEGA

a power balance; the outcome was not black, white, or gray. But I do believe that what it manifested was a swerve in the direction of an altogether new cultural construct.

Something that I've learned from all of these experiences is that we are always influenced and determined by a dominant way of seeing things. But to be critical of this dominance within a specific practice, which is what most of us always want to do anyway, we need to do so from within as practitioners of such practice. We can't just stand there, reflecting on it passively or taking an outsider's perspective; you cannot really walk away from the cultural constructs you are embedded into, no matter how much you disagree with them.

NDA I'm curious how you dealt with all these questions in the studio format, where you must move beyond analysis and critique into specific design proposals.

JS We did what studios are best suited to do: respond to intellectual demands through design by engaging a specific set of circumstances and needs. The "design mode" of research and pedagogy gives us a unique perspective and understanding of society: its history, its present, and its possible futures. In all these studios I made sure that we amplified and diversified the students' perspectives on all the areas of knowledge, art, and politics that converged in relation to our problem at hand. But I also made it so that they had no alternative to confronting their proposed interventions other than by addressing these issues through *exclusively architectural* means.

I think that broadening our understanding should not be confused with studio formats prevalent today in which architecture is just a support scaffolding to principally address topics provided by the field of technology or the politics of the humanities. I believe that making architecture the *inescapable protagonist* of an architectural education is today an ethical imperative. All these other topics should be a part of the questions we ask ourselves in the studio but not the ultimate goal.

NDA In a recent conversation with Sarah Whiting for *Pairs* 01, she pointed out that design teaching was essentially about dialogue because discourse advances through conversation, regardless of the form it takes. When I reflect on some of the theory seminars that you have taught recently, I remember them as exactly that: agglomerations of concepts, ideas, and references in the process of finding shape; propositions, questions, and observations more than definitive answers. Perhaps what was most refreshing about the experience was seeing how we can revisit the history of our discipline and, by virtue of the way we compose and connect its parts, find new and useful ways of learning from it. It is perhaps the closest approach to Aby Warburg's methodology that I encountered in my years as a student.

Maybe because you are not a historian but rather a designer with a passion for history, you are constantly trying to understand why a given architect made certain decisions. I think more than ever this is a worthy undertaking. It enables us to look at the history of our discipline as a set of exercises performed by people trying to make the right choice given their priorities amid complicated and often contradictory constraints. And it gives us the hindsight to evaluate the consequences or impact of these decisions in time. With so many anti–status quo priorities implicit in discussions in schools of architecture today, this feels incredibly useful.

JS   Yes, that's the way teaching the history of architecture should be approached in a school of architecture! One of the pedagogical contributions that I am most proud of is the work that Howard Burns and I did at the GSD to create the course Buildings, Texts, and Contexts (BTC), which was then amplified by the contributions of K. Michael Hays and Wilfried Wang at the turn of the millennium. We essentially broke away from the idea of the survey course as a way to teach architectural history at the graduate level, since we thought it was unnecessary, in favor of the approach you are describing.

We imposed surveys as a prerequisite to admission to the program and developed a way to teach history that was specifically conceived and designed for graduate architecture programs. Until that point, history in architecture schools was taught in the same way as in fine arts schools. We thought this was not the best approach because the courses were too distant from the studios and lost all relation to the design process, which is ultimately one of the chief concerns of our education.

Howard and I argued that the history of architecture in a professional school had to be taught jointly and on an equal level by one architect and one historian. We were the first to try this out, and the result was fantastic. Though we started it at the GSD, I think it did have some repercussions in other graduate programs across the country.

Each week we taught a case, usually a single building, and every once in a while a text. On Tuesday, I would start off by looking at the building in itself. On Thursday, Howard would then bring in more of the historical context. But he would do so by extending out from the piece of architecture (or text) under scrutiny and going only as far as necessary to hypothesize what the actual process of design had been. So, we would look at the building from the inside out, trying to reconstruct, in a somewhat speculative way, what was going through the mind of the architect in the creative process. This, by the way, is another example of how one can position oneself within what one is studying, analyzing, or interpreting.

It was a total success because it really made the cases useful and accessible to us as architects tasked with our own creative endeavors, with our own need to respond to the myriad of conditions in our context in order to give shape to a specific building or space.

NDA   Did your interest in the "marginal" expressions of Western architecture percolate into the list of cases?

JS   Of course! One of the first things we did was incorporate cases like El Escorial or the Mosque of Córdoba as breakthrough dislocations within Western culture. These were buildings that were discussed in conventional courses but always in passing. Much of what I've shared with you today was less clear to me back then, but this urge to push these cases toward the center was there, I guess.

By placing these types of buildings in equal position among canonical exemplars, we make them act as moments of epiphany in our understanding of the cultural dynamics of architecture. The mosque was a building done entirely with Roman technology and Roman architectural component pieces, and yet, a complete invention for an emerging religious and political power. It was a type of building that had never been seen anywhere else. It was also a building that underwent expansions and modifications across centuries, adapting itself to rituals and a religious culture in evolution. Its later history is actually its transformation from mosque to cathedral, which I think is an extraordinary cultural phenomenon to witness and which deals with many issues that are resurfacing in our contemporary concerns.

NDA   I think our generation feels an urgency to reinvent many of the conventions that we take for granted in order to respond to new conditions that we are alarmed by. And I think this holds true whether we talk about the way we build, practice, foster community, or govern.

To me, the events that unfolded around the issue of police brutality in the US last year are a very clear example of this. But they also showed that the desire to dismantle and reassemble anew or to radically restructure something is very complex and nuanced. It is ultimately an act of negotiation between a new set of aspirations and an establishment that it is often at odds with.

Do you think there are tangible ways to use the sort of scholarship we have discussed today to seriously deal with issues like the representation of cultural minorities or marginalized segments of society in our fields?

JS   Well, I'd like to first say that the culture of minorities and marginalized groups—in any society—are strains that are as much a part of that culture as the dominant strains are. They may be distorted, diminished, subjugated, or repressed, as they usually are. They may also enjoy uncontrollable success, as they do in some exceptional cases. But they are an inextricable component in the larger cultural pot.

I think that the most productive way to effect positive change is to understand from within how all these strains exist within the larger whole. In what conditions and degrees of dependency, freedom, and repression do they operate and interact with one another?

By understanding these mechanisms, we can put them at our service to transform the processes of change in positive ways. Can we build a cultural condition in which the dominance of one strain is transformed into the collective interaction of many diverse strains? I believe this is an aspiration that we can only hope to achieve by better understanding what has brought us to where we are today.

To answer your question, I think we can look at cases that help us better understand these processes. We can look at how marginalized strains within a dominant culture have been able to operate with diverse efficiencies and degrees of success. For instance, I am currently trying to spell out the difference between architecture and music for my course.

Why that pair? Because I want us to assess in my upcoming seminar why Black culture in the US has registered such a meager impact in one—architecture—versus such extraordinary influence in the other.

These are two fundamental and universal cultural practices. Each of them has distinctive modes of production based on basic and inescapable scientific and natural phenomena: gravity, sound waves, the human need for shelter, the urge to by actually returning to a classical vocabulary. And when this made it to the scene, it caught on like wildfire, reigniting the pendulum of fashion. It soon led us to encounters with the equally reactionary and fragmentary discourse of Deconstructivism, which became dissipated through the later fascination with new technologies, materials, and digital tools. All in all, architecture disappeared as a central topic for almost two decades in our discipline.

I think it's interesting and exciting that we are in fact seeing renewed interest in talking about architecture itself and in engaging the topic of history. I think what is new about this moment is not really the social and political dimension of architecture. This was something we were already heatedly discussing in the 1960s. Rodolfo and I were pursuing our master's degrees at UC Berkeley back then, so there was no escaping this!

What is truly new is the determination—the need—to treat this not just at a conceptual level, but at an operational one. That is what I perceive we have relative consensus about right now: the desire to get our hands into it and make architecture change. Reflecting upon the topic and understanding it better isn't enough anymore. Your generation seems to want to take these understandings of history and change everything. It's about action now.

¿A ti qué te parece, Nicolás?

JORGE SILVETTI WITH NICOLÁS DELGADO ÁLCEGA

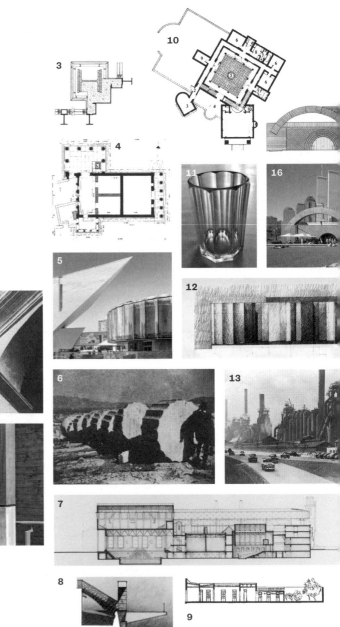

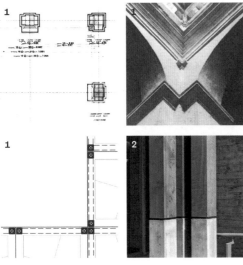

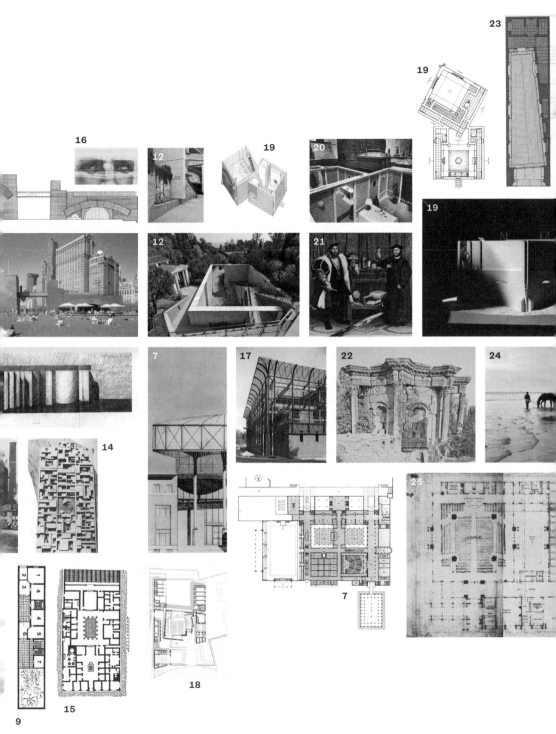

123

symbolize, to communicate emotionally, etc. They also have specific relations to material infrastructure and modes of transmission.

So, why is it that jazz became the most extraordinary and truly original American cultural product? Can we gain something from reading it as a synthesis of multiple strains, sources, and directions, whether they came from minority or canonical histories? I think that by discerning between the particular combinations of factors that come together to create music and architecture, we can better understand how power operates in these different practices. With what intensity do dominant forms of power register in each one of these cultural practices, and what does that tell us about the different ways in which we can affect American culture through them?

This is a great case, because we have the last century-and-a-half to look into. And I do think it can help us develop feasible, grounded strategies through which to address many of the issues that surfaced in 2020 in our discipline over the next decade.

NDA   I'd like to end with a question about the changing role of history in our discipline. You came up in a period when history was being truly rediscovered for architecture as modernism met its demise. I'm curious what you think about the discussions being had about history today among designers in schools of architecture? There seems to be a renewed interest in talking about architecture and history, in unpacking and problematizing certain histories with all their political and social implications for the present.

JS   What we were doing in the mid-1960s and 1970s was really rediscovering history for architecture, which had been buried by modernism for decades. But it was a very conceptual search, deeply rooted in philosophy, anthropology, and other domains. We were trying to explain to ourselves how architecture really worked, culturally and socially. And I think that was the best contribution that postmodernism made to our discipline. Through analogies with language, we tried to explain how signification and meaning works in our discipline and how you can structure them into the creative process.

In a way, it was the first pass at this return to history, and I think it achieved a base level understanding of these concepts that today is quite mainstream. But that return to history was trivialized by interpreting it literally in an operative way,

Sara Hendren

with Elisa Ngan

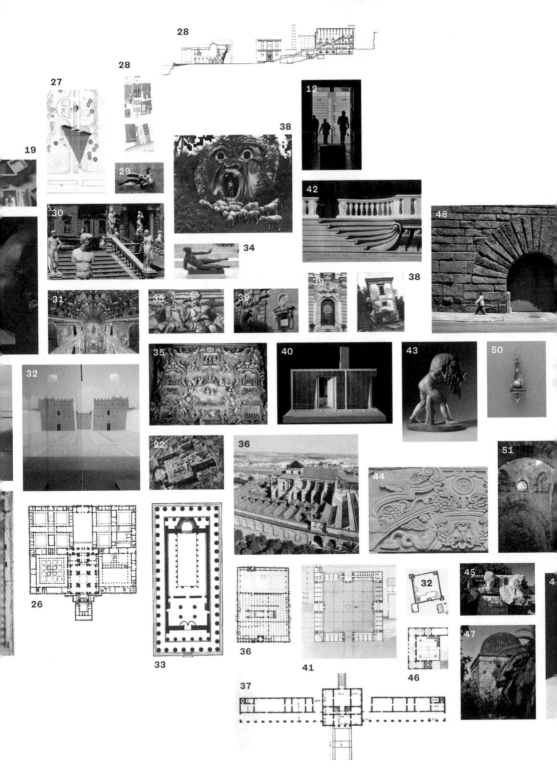

LABYRINTH OF AFFINITIES

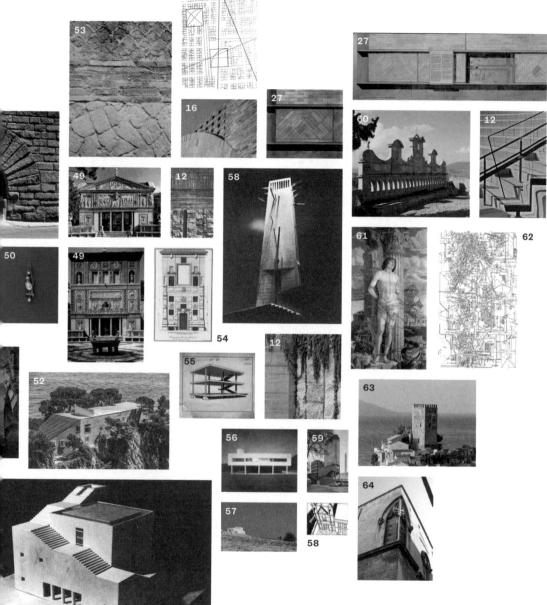

1 Chiostro del Bramante, c. 1500, D. Bramante
2 Benton Museum of Art, 2020, J. Silvetti
3 US Courthouse Chicago, 1963, L.M. van der Rohe
4 Erechtheion, 421–406 B.C., Mnesicles (attributed), Phidias
5 Denver Art Museum, 2021, J. Silvetti
6 Le Corbusier at the Parthenon, 1911
7 Carnegie Mellon University Center, 1987, R. Machado and J. Silvetti
8 Piazza Dante, 1990, J. Silvetti
9 Typical Argentinian Casa Chorizo
10 House in Lake Pergusa, 1983, J. Silvetti
11 Fluted Glass Tumbler, collection of J. Silvetti
12 Getty Villa, 2007, J. Silvetti
13 Pittsburgh Steel Mills
14 Free University of Berlin, 1963, Candilis, Josic, Woods and Schiedhelm
15 House of Pansa, 2nd cent. B.C.
16 Robert F. Wagner, Jr. Park, 1996, J. Silvetti
17 Princeton University Parking Structure, 1991, J. Silvetti
18 Church and Parrochial Complex, 2007, J. Silvetti
19 Taberna Anticipas Formae, 1983, J. Silvetti
20 Kramer Residence, 1981, R. Machado and J. Silvetti
21 The Ambassadors, 1533, Hans Holbein The Younger
22 Temple of Venus (Baalbek), 3rd cent. B.C.
23 Portantina Showroom, 1986, R. Machado and J. Silvetti
24 From the series Río de la Plata, 1994, M. Zimmermann
25 First Church of Christ, Scientist, 1910, B.R. Maybeck
26 El Escorial, 1584 J.B. de Toledo, J. de Herrera
27 Cranbrook Academy Entrance Gate, 1991, J. Silvetti
28 The Steps of Providence, 1978, J. Silvetti
29 La Rivière, 1938, A. Maillol
30 Fontana Pretoria, 1554, F. Camilliani
31 Cappella Palatina, 12th cent. A.D.
32 Qasr Al Muwaiji Research Center and Museum, 2012, J. Silvetti

33 Parthenon as Byzantine Church, 6th cent. A.D.
34 L'air, 1938, A. Maillol
35 Oratorio di San Lorenzo, 1706, G. Serpotta
36 Mosque-Cathedral of Córdoba, 8th–16th cent. A.D.
37 Villa Emo, 16th cent. A.D., A. Palladio
38 Sacro Bosco, 16th cent. A.D., Pirro Ligorio (attributed), Simone Moschino
39 Palazzo Zuccari, 16th cent. A.D., F. Zuccari
40 Gateway for Venice, 1990, J. Silvetti
41 Landing of The Sperone, 1988, J. Silvetti
42 Marble staircase (Chiesa di Santo Stefano al Ponte), 1574, B. Buontalenti
43 Young Satyr Wearing Theater Mask of Silenus, 1st cent. A.D.
44 Ruins of San Ignacio Miní, 17th cent. A.D.
45 Temple of Apollo (Didyma), 300 B.C.–200 A.D.
46 House in Tunisia, 1976, J. Silvetti
47 Chiesa di San Glovanni degli Eremiti, 1132
48 Allegheny County Courthouse, 1888, H.H. Richardson
49 Casina Pio IV, 1562, P. Ligorio
50 Baroque Pearls, 16th–17th cent. A.D.
51 Chiesa di San Cataldo, 1154
52 Casa Malaparte, 1938, A. Libera
53 Image of Detail From Villa Adriana, J. Silvetti
54 Palazzetto Zuccari, 16th cent. A.D., F. Zuccari
55 Maison Dom-Ino, 1914–1915, Le Corbusier
56 Villa Savoye, 1931, Le Corbusier, P. Jeanneret
57 View of Djerba (Tunisia), J. Silvetti
58 Four Public Squares and Tower of Leonforte, 1983, J. Silvetti
59 Engineering Building at Leicester Universit,1963, J. Stirling
60 Granfonte di Leonforte, 165, M. Smiriglio
61 San Sebastiano, 1480, A. Mantegna
62 Micromega Drawing, 1979, D. Libeskind
63 Castello di Brolo, 10th cent. A.D.
64 Palazzo Alliata di Pietratagliata, 1473

125

Nearly Me Breast Prosthetic

On Help

ELISA NGAN   When the GSD thinks about disability, it's usually in the context of the built environment: ramps and code, bathrooms and grab bars, etc. We encounter disability primarily as a given set of functional system requirements.

On the other hand, you teach a design studio where students make bespoke products for and with clients who have disabilities. In this case, disability is intimate.

This is an image of Ruth Handler holding up her Nearly Me prosthetic, a product designed for people who had breast cancer and underwent a mastectomy. She invented both the Nearly Me and Barbie dolls.

The way she so proudly cradles the soft, blobby, innocuous prosthetic in this image inspires confidence in its worth, yet Audre Lorde positions Ruth Handler's prosthetic more critically in *The Cancer Journals*. Have you read the book?

The first version of the Americans with Disabilities Act (ADA) was passed in 1990. In 2020, the law marked its thirtieth anniversary, and questions about disability were left off the decennial census for the first time since the ADA's enactment. US federal programs use census population data for budgetary purposes.

SARA HENDREN   Yeah, and the most memorable story from that book for me is when she wakes up in the post-op moment with a new body. The sun is shining, and she finds herself alive, having survived something really terrifying and feeling beautiful, actually. She puts on one earring for the day, and she's got this beautiful asymmetry happening that she decides to just lean fully into.

And she shows up at the doctor's office, and the nurse says to her, "Oh, you're not wearing the replacement part," this Nearly Me, this soft prosthesis of the breast that makes the wearer's chest appear symmetrical again.

And she says, "I'm good, I don't need it."

And the nurse says, "Well, it's bad morale for the office if you don't."

EN   Ha, yep, yikes.

Ruth Handler looks directly at the camera and positions her light-skin-toned Nearly Me breast prosthetic in front of her left breast over her blue blazer, 1976.

SARA HENDREN WITH ELISA NGAN

SH   So we can say, "Oh, yes, all prosthetics are biopolitical in that they pose a choice to the user," right? A choice about what the user wants to wear and perform and all that arrives in an object. But here, Lorde is taking it one step further to say, "Prosthetics are not just biopolitical in the sense of what I choose or don't choose but in the meaning that other people are making of me and my body. And I don't get to opt in or opt out of those kinds of ideas." Of course, that's true in the racialized sense and in the gendered sense and also of replacement parts and prosthetics.

EN   Lorde and Handler are surprisingly similar: Both are strong women. Both are pioneers in their very particular careers. Both are trying to define not only the feminine but how to *be* feminine. Handler was inspired to invent the Barbie doll by watching her own daughter role-play a future version of herself through her dolls. It was a speculative prop to practice the feminine. And here, her Nearly Me prosthetic extends and preserves those same normative ideals.

      Knowing this story as we do now and knowing all those who opt in to Nearly Me today, are their actions antithetical to the work of feminists and feminism?

SH   No, life is not as simple as that. In the way that fictional characters and nonfictional characters invite us into their points of view, it's really just about thinking that if we were sitting there in that waiting room with Audre Lorde, what resources would we marshal to make that choice and all those choices that would be available to us?

      There are lots of reasons people opt in to replacement parts of all kinds, but are we clear that the decisions that we make are not purely the inherited decisions about who we think we should be—the "ideal woman," and so on? Do we have a rich enough figuration of what is human in our mind's eye to ask, "I'm going to imagine what my best life looks like. What are the tasks that are meaningful to me"?

EN   Personally, I had to ask myself those same questions when I decided to pursue architecture. Choosing a collaborative and communication-heavy profession felt like choosing a life full of unnecessary frustrations and failures. After all, why would you want to constantly do the thing you struggle with and can't improve or control, something that is only going to get worse over time at a rate that you don't know and can't anticipate?

Elisa has severe bilateral hearing loss and wears hearing aids. Hearing aids function poorly in environments with loud background noise, and people with hearing loss have challenges processing speech when there are multiple speakers.

At the end of the day, as much as the pressure to choose and "inherit" those narratives existed in my disability and my prosthetics, the tasks I found meaningful existed outside of that world.

SH   Exactly. Our ideas of wholeness, our ideas of functionality, our ideas of femininity, masculinity, are deeply tied up with these replacement parts. It includes everyone, no matter the body that they're in. When you are extending your body with reading glasses or orthotic shoes or outsourcing some brain functions to your smartphone so that you can keep your mind for other kinds of decision-making, all of that might be thought of in a big canopy of prosthetics … and none of those things are so simple as a functional object.

So, it's really interesting to think about prosthetics in the realm of design, which hinges on narratives that are around them, precede them, and follow them, and all the ways that we're making sense of the world, not just in what's available to us functionally but in the kinds of stories that are being told by the things we opt in to and the things we opt out of.

I've been interested for a long time in design and disability. And as you said, in architecture or any design context, it tends to proceed from the logic of rehabilitation engineering, that whole field of rehabilitating the body. You can see it arriving right here in this idea of the replacement breast, the return to the "nearly me": maybe not quite but almost there. You can see it arriving in the performative, identity way of what a normative woman's body looks like in that femininity, in that symmetry, and so on. We see the persuasive story being told about replacement parts, how it's really not just functional, but it's actually about identity too. And that's interesting because that's where we look at design as doing what we'd call "biopolitical work."

EN   It can be hard for designers to navigate how to do this biopolitical work. In 2020, over 60 percent of people with disabilities in the United States are unemployed.[1] How can we manage the ethics of research when working with people with disabilities to minimize undue burden?

SH   Any of us, depending on the kinds of agency we have and the hours in the day, will do things because we are intrinsically motivated to build certain kinds of relationships. I want students to feel liberated to express interest, to ask politely, to pay for people's time when they can. But yeah, my students

Minimizing undue burden on vulnerable communities is a principle of distributive justice theory. In a US academic context, the principle comes into play when considering the ethics of research and is managed by an institutional review board specifically developed to protect the human rights of research subjects.

[1] Bureau of Labor Statistics, United States Department of Labor, "Persons with a Disability: Labor Force Characteristics—2020," news release, February 24, 2021, https://www.bls.gov/news.release/pdf/disabl.pdf.

SARA HENDREN WITH ELISA NGAN

struggle with the same thing. They feel an instantaneous sense that transactionally they're getting more out of it because they're getting a grade or they're learning something.

But what I've learned is that unless folks are taxing their interviewees inappropriately, most people are only too happy to talk about themselves and about their lives.

Honestly, Elisa, I think there's almost a neoliberal creep into that logic, the logic of the market in our lives. People frame it as a student who "wins," in other words, and so therefore someone else has to "lose." It makes us think of all our interactions as transactional and market-driven. Do you see how zero sum that is?

EN   True.

SH   Again, paying people for their time is important if it's a big extended project or something, but people can say no. And I think you can feel confident that lots of times those interactions are built on something other than gaining or losing. If you only seek out experiences where you're on the offering end and never on the receiving end, you miss out. And I don't think you want a future in which you're always trying to avoid that position. I think you want a future in which, when the day comes, you're more dependent than you were before—this is a flourishing, happy life too. It's as simple as that.

"Crip time" is a concept in critical disability studies. On an individual level, it expresses how those with disabilities must allocate time differently due to the unique needs of their bodies. At a systems level, it speaks to a tension with the standard eight-hour workday and its assumptions and expectations about how long things should take.

EN   Well, the transactional is hard to get past as someone who lives on crip time: the give, the take, the exchange, the energy.

SH   I'm curious if you're using web captioners or some of those automation tools on a regular basis.

EN   I don't. I tried, but they're not *nearly* good enough for real-time. I also don't fully identify as disabled or Deaf, so I don't see myself as someone who needs captions by default. I think I'm doing fine, but I also know that I don't know what normal is.

SH   Your story actually reminds me of a friend and former colleague of mine who was also mainstreamed. She got an electrical engineering degree with no accommodations, did lipreading, exhausted herself doing that, but also thought of it as normal, and was raised with a strong sense that she should be normal. It was a journey through grad school to ask for the interpreter, and it's precisely this thing where she did not know how to identify as D/deaf, much less as disabled.

NEARLY ME BREAST PROSTHETIC

Deafness is both a culture and a condition. Identifying as uppercase *D* Deaf indicates that one is part of a culture that shares specific beliefs, values, and norms about what it means to be deaf and a common language, such as American Sign Language. Identifying as lowercase *d* deaf indicates that one relates to deafness primarily as an audiological condition rather than a cultural one.

Yeah, people assume that just because you are disabled, you identify as disabled, and you know you're disabled. But depending on how you entered into disability, this is not always true. Your friend's story resonates with me because, yeah, our disability is just one part of our total experiences and personalities, and these things are always evolving.

I imagine this ability to push our disability to the peripheral is more possible for disabilities that are invisible to others. This can create some interesting situations. For a couple years, I tried to find people with hearing loss who did not identify as a person who had a "problem," people like your friend. It was really hard. When I found them they were so excited because they were so lonely.

I realized that you have to identify with a problem to be found, connected, and helped. If there is a tension or a misalignment between how you identify your problem and how the world identifies your problem, it can be one of the most painful sources of suffering and anger. I think about the classification of problems, which is essentially the practice of diagnosis, all the time. The diagnosis itself is double-edged. It gives a reason, but it is a reason that is reductive to the coping experience of the person with a disability.

To bring dimensionality to someone with a disability, to counter that reductiveness of diagnosis so that we can enable a different set of possibilities … I feel like this is a socially embodied learning that is powerful and incredibly special in the studio you teach. I wish there was more of it at the GSD. In my own MDE studio there were various opportunities to design for someone with a disability, but as a designer who has a disability, it was extremely uncomfortable to witness how various projects got done. At times it felt like everyone patting themselves on the back for their own altruistic genius. This is not specific to MDE; this is the design performance in general. How many awards have we seen given to a stair-climbing wheelchair? A hearing aid that is also a piece of jewelry? A Swiss-army-knife cane?

"Inspiration porn" describes the practice of representing people with disabilities as exceptional or heroic. It is a common marketing tactic that perpetuates harmful stereotypes about people who live with disability. It allows those who do not have a disability to feel more comfortable about their abled bodies by abreacting their pity and guilt into a positive form.

At UC Berkeley, where I went for my undergrad, I was able to take a class with Raymond Lifchez. He used to teach a pretty radical architecture studio in the 1970s, one similar to yours, where people with disabilities came in as clients. He observed as a professor that one of the first barriers to get over as a designer and student in this space is just being able to genuinely interact with someone who has a disability in the first place. He positioned designing for disability as a relational exercise instead of the paternalistic one we see so often today.

132

SH   Yeah, so, my students designed and built a ramp for wheelchair dancing, right? So, Alice Sheppard, this wheelchair dancer, comes to class, introduces what she wants, does some dancing, then we get right to prototyping, and so on. All of the prototyping and the energy … our eyes are trained on this common purpose, the scale model, and the dimensions.

But really, there's all this work happening between and among those people, where the students who are nondisabled are looking at Alice and thinking, "That's not what I thought a wheelchair is used for." And Alice becomes a round character, not flat. She is not synonymous with the chair, and the wheelchair-using part of her life is not the entirety of her life. She has tastes and senses of humor, and she can play. All of those things that we think we know are true, but if you have not interacted with somebody who uses a wheelchair, you might imagine that theirs is a whole medically tragic existence, right?

I hardly have to say much of anything for them to get it because the relationship that is being built by the trial of a common task is this natural convivial result. It's better than just having Alice across the table narrating her life. The building of it speaks past all of your awkwardness and all of your second-guessing and all of your wondering.

Audre Lorde called herself a warrior poet, wrote a lot of poetry, and believed in the poetic gesture. She shows us just how dimensional and multidirectional these prosthetic meanings are, complicating a really compressed and simplified narrative about where disability starts and stops. I mean, people have a very linear logic that you, as a designer, when working on a "problem" of disability, are just trying to create the structures of the world in a more accessible or useful way. Yes, it is that, but really what you see when you dig one level deeper is the civic and common human stakes for finding a world bumping up against bodies and all the meaning that's made therein.

EN   Even in the everyday when you walk around. I remember there was someone who was blind walking down the echoey hallway in the Science Center asking for some direction into the air, and we were all just sitting there frozen at our tables because we weren't quite sure what to do. On one level, there's this very intellectual concern, "How do I design? What do I do with the choices that I'm able to make for someone else?" And then when you're confronted with the actual interaction, there's a unique set of intimate problems.

133

SH   Yeah, it's so true. How do you talk about it? How do you offer or not offer help? That's such a subtle thing that you're describing. I'm imagining my students at all their desks five, 10 years from now, and when the moment arises to call the Association for the Blind, wherever they are, they don't hesitate to pick up the phone, because they think, "I got through that awkward conversation"—like Raymond Lifchez talked about—"I got through that first awkward conversation and the second one and the third one, and I built a relationship, and I'm going to make peace with that feeling," right?

Nobody ever teaches us this stuff unless you just really build relationships to do so. So, that encounter that you just described, I see that all the time. I think that should surely be a bigger part of our education. Danielle Allen, political theorist at the Edmond J. Safra Center for Ethics at Harvard, calls it "participatory readiness," this idea that at the end of our education, we're ready to embark on conversations with people very unlike ourselves, and we're more likely to do so rather than continuing to back away.

EN   That reminds me of a quote from Lifchez's book as well: "… for the ways that architecture enters the lives of people, people we know and love and others for whom we have not yet learned to care."[2] Design is meaningful work. Your work is meaningful to me, and I'm sure to many others who have disabilities or love those with one or several. For you though, why do you do it? What's important to you?

[2]   Raymond Lifchez *Rethinking Architecture: Design Students and Physically Disabled People* (Berkeley: University of California Press, 1987), xii.

SH   For me, it's really important to be both critical in a scholarly sense and also to keep pointing to modes of repair. The pragmatic designer in me needs to say, "Look over here, look at this really interesting thing." It's never as simple as, "Here's this thing that you think is so great. I'm going to tell you how it's not so great." I don't take that much joy in letting that be the end of the story. I read all that stuff; it's really important work. But for me, I need that practitioner-pragmatic bent to also point to repair.

EN   Yes! Repair is so important when you depend on an object to survive, yet it's such a neglected part of the design lifecycle. It is literally the first thing I think when I wake up: do I need hearing aid batteries?

SH   That is exactly right. The condition of misfitting and disability is a reminder of how bodied the body is. So, in other words, no critique in the abstract will ever suffice. We can be critical all day long about the supply chain and manufacturing and all the conditions under which those technologies have come to take over our lives, but, I mean, I do have to get up and out the door the next day.

And as a mother of a person with Down syndrome, I can't afford the luxury of just throwing rocks at what designers do. My son loves the auto-complete text that an AI is serving him on Gmail … which is then monetizing all of his data. I don't love the economic model of that, but I want that for him, because I think he's going to want it. I mean, I'm watching him want it, right? So I can't afford to be, again, only in the "unmasking" role of the scholar. I have to see where it's done well.

EN   Do you ever worry that the technology is going to leave him behind in some ways that we can't see?

SH   Well, there's never been any organizing so that folks in that position are not left behind. He would have been institutionalized a generation ago, I mean, utterly warehoused and managed. So, I'm not optimistic that a culture is going to organize around and prioritize developmental disability. That's why an expanded figuration of the human, the body, and its needs is at the heart of my work: because I can imagine a future in which it's okay to get old. It's also okay to be slower, the way he is. It's okay to ask for help in public, and you're more likely to offer help in public, and to make room in your workplace, and to send your kids to school with kids like mine. So, I think that technology is just one little vector in an entire disposition toward difference and help—which is really what's at stake.

Lyndon Neri

with Nicolás Delgado Álcega

Sketches for a Scarpa Show

On Placing Ourselves in the Field

NICOLÁS DELGADO ÁLCEGA   Let's start by talking about the work you are doing with MAXXI in Rome. From the material you sent over, I got the sense you were using the Carlo Scarpa archive at the museum to develop a new reading of his work. Is the intent to curate a selection of drawings for a show based on your perspective?

LYNDON NERI   We are working on the fourth in a series of exhibitions that happen every year at MAXXI where a designer is invited to look into the archive of the museum. The primary goal is for the designers to glean from it and present what inspires them to the public.

We started by making it very clear that we wanted to focus on the more architectural material, since we are architects. We quickly narrowed it down to two architects in MAXXI's archive: Aldo Rossi and Carlo Scarpa. Although Scarpa and Rossi have been widely exhibited—even in just the last decade—we thought there was something original that we could bring to the table through this show. Thankfully the archive was all digitized, since we were not able to travel to it due to COVID-19 restrictions. It wasn't the same as seeing and touching it physically, but it allowed us to quickly hone in on Scarpa.

Above all, we felt we should look for new revelations in the archive. Our practice deals a lot with Rossi's notion of the urban artifact: the idea that the act of building is part of the way a city gives continuity to its collective memory. That is important to us, especially in light of what's been happening here in Shanghai in the last 20 years. But the Rossi archive was focused on different facets of the earlier work.

Soon after looking through everything, we started to hone in on Scarpa's domestic spaces and the unique way in which he understood the concept of the threshold. The archive has a lot of material that refers to this. We will be looking, of course, at the built work but also at a lot of the unbuilt houses and other projects that have been perhaps more overlooked.

NDA   I'm curious if there is a link between your selection of Scarpa and the interest that you and Rossana Hu have in the concept of the *Gesamtkunstwerk*. Scarpa had a kind of connection with Josef Hoffmann and other exponents of this tradition. In my opinion, although he is influenced by these ideas, they come through his work differently. From a superficial perspective, Scarpa seems to be more concerned with the incomplete piecing together of fragments. What I perceive as total in his work is a weaving of independent fragments into a total composition, not the idea of designing everything.

LN   Yes, yes, that's a very good point. But it's the opposite of what we feel Scarpa's relevance is to our work. What interests us about Carlo Scarpa is this understanding of thresholds. So, the show is not so focused on *Gesamtkunstwerk*, because we don't see him as that type of individual. We are working with the way he dealt with tension from a spatial, visual, and tectonic perspective.

I think people often see our work and make the connection to Scarpa on a more superficial level. For example, people look at the Aranya Art Center, where a water duct travels through the main atrium with bronze detailing, and immediately say, "Well that's natural, Neri&Hu loves Carlo Scarpa and his craftsmanship." And they miss the point, because what we take from Scarpa is this act of trying to strip elements to their most essential form. We mainly look at Carlo Scarpa as an inspiration from a spatial point of view rather than as a craftsman, even in the details.

NDA   The use of an architectural element like the threshold in Scarpa's work to propose an alternative reading of his oeuvre seems to me closely linked to your perspective as a practitioner. What do you think Rossana and yourself are uniquely equipped to do as architects, in stating a position through a museum exhibit, as opposed to a curator or historian?

LN   Well, we are actually working very closely with a curator at MAXXI, Domitilla Dardi. It has been a very fruitful collaboration because we were initially very focused on the narrative of the exhibition, and less concerned with the curatorial consistency of our argument. And Domitilla has been instrumental in bringing that kind of clarity and robustness to the table.

Sketches by Lyndon Neri for *Traversing Thresholds*, an exhibition opening November 2021 at MAXXI in Rome.

SKETCHES FOR A SCARPA SHOW

I think what we offer here, Nicolás, is the capacity to do something that is very obviously an interpretation. And we are doing that through the capacity to shape space and materials in a new way within the walls of the museum. We are proposing a reading of the work through a series of spaces that highlight a distinct way in which Scarpa was dealing with the threshold. What you are seeing in this document is a list of some of those: the datum line, the eroded corner, the expanded field, etc.

So, for example, when you enter, the opening room deals with hardware; the pulling, pushing, and touching involved in the hardware that Scarpa designed to deal with the sense of entry. You then move on to a room that deals with the eroded corner, where we made a sort of chamber to be by yourself. Scarpa made a lot of these moments in his work, where you enter a space that can't really hold more than one person, where you have to get out to let the next person in.

Ultimately, I think we are proposing alternative ways of reading architectural devices that are very present in Scarpa's work. This is what we have been looking for through the sketches you are seeing. Hopefully by articulating them spatially in an alternative way, we can all of a sudden make the work more obvious and legible to the audience.

NDA   What are you doing differently from the way Scarpa might have done it?

LN   It's totally different. I mean, just to give you an example, we are collaborating with the microfiber manufacturer Alcantara to see how we can use their material for the show. And we are approaching it in quite a radical way. We didn't want to use just fabric, so we will take all of their old catalogs and will splice and stack them to make them into bricks. They're old catalogs, so they are already part of history. So just like mud, we are going to compress them, make bricks, and then stack them. And then we will take the Alcantara felt itself and use it as grout, which is the most important thing. In a way, it's about producing something that is closely related to both the sacred and the profane.

We are working with our present reality but bringing to it a certain resonance with Carlo Scarpa. He worked on a number of projects that were not just about precious materials, and he used pretty poor materials to create what I consider to be a new sublime. In *Critique of Pure Reason*, Kant proposes the idea that pursuing the immensity of possibility is so much better than pursuing the solution. And I think that is a new sublime we read in Scarpa's work and are looking for

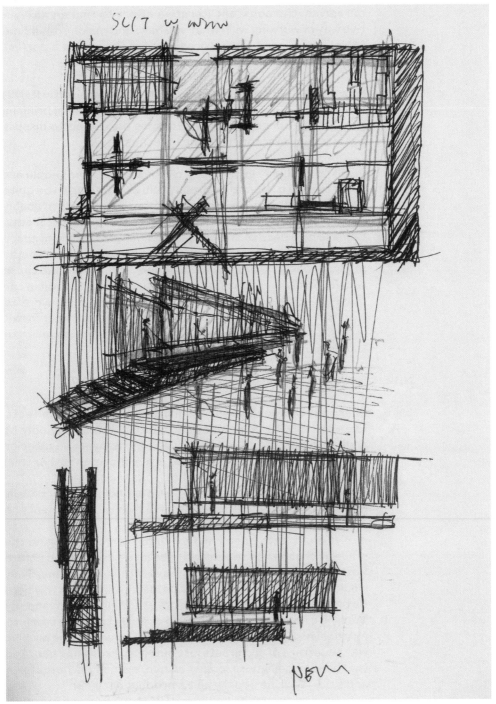

Sketches by Lyndon Neri for *Traversing Thresholds*, an exhibition opening November 2021 at MAXXI in Rome.

SKETCHES FOR A SCARPA SHOW

ourselves: the constant iterative effort to find an alternative way of working with what you have and making it sublime. I think the Gavina Bookstore facade in Bologna is a perfect example of that.

NDA   How do you think your interpretation will be received in Italy? I saw in the documents you shared that you will also be bringing the Chinese concept of *Zhōngjiān* into the exhibit to discuss Scarpa's understanding of the threshold.

LN   It will be good to see. I'm very curious about how people are going to take it. Domitilla already told us it's going to be quite controversial because there will be two camps. It's probably a good thing that we are not Italian. We are coming from a Chinese perspective and bringing a different reading of space and threshold that is lodged in our own experience. People might find it amusing because of this. I do think that those who love Scarpa might find our spatial interpretation in the museum to be a watered-down version of his skill as a craftsman. But that's a risk we are willing to take, because our intent is to show him as much more than a craftsman—as an architect in his own right.

NDA   Do you think Scarpa is generally seen otherwise?

LN   Scarpa is well-loved by a small group of Italian architects. Even globally, he does enjoy recognition, but I'd say only by a small group. He tends to be seen by many as an interior designer, someone who is focused on composition rather than on the design of the elements that make the composition. The conversation tends to be around his work being proportionally and aesthetically pleasing, not so much on the statements he was making with it.

It must have been hard for him. I can only imagine the struggle that he had to deal with. I believe Gio Ponti and Ettore Sottsass were in their younger days at this same time. They would look at Scarpa and say, "Well, he's an architect trying to do product design." The architects would look at him and say, "Well, he's not really so much of an architect; he's just an interior designer glorified as an architect." I mean, in the archive we saw letters of architects just outright dismissing him. And the interior designers looked at him, even in his hometown, and said, "Well, he's really just a product designer."

So even though he had joined CIAM and engaged in conversations with Le Corbusier, Marcel Breuer, Louis Kahn, and

Sketches by Lyndon Neri for *Traversing Thresholds*, an exhibition opening November 2021 at MAXXI in Rome.

SKETCHES FOR A SCARPA SHOW

many other figures from that time, he was never taken seriously. However, we argue that there were moments through which he was influencing a lot of architects, which should make his work more broadly relevant to our discipline.

NDA   I think Scarpa remains quite cryptic for many. I remember as an undergraduate student trying to understand why I was being referred to Scarpa's work and not being able to extract a larger logic from the moments and details that images relate. Perhaps this was partly because his work particularly requires being seen in person. But I think that's a big part of the challenge with Scarpa and with comparing him to figures whose work had much clearer manifestos or positions behind them.

One of the things I find interesting about Scarpa now is that he was a person that was reflecting early on about what modernism was in relation to the rest of architectural history and different architectural traditions. And I think his reading was very mature for his moment because it had distance from the dogmatism of the period. If you look at some of the things Scarpa was interested in and looked up to, like Josef Hoffman and the Vienna Secession, many of them belonged to a much more fertile period of modernism, right? I see Scarpa as someone with an outsider's perspective to his time.

LN   Yes, we are going to be giving a lecture that accompanies the opening of the show, and this is actually something we will deal with in the introduction. Scarpa was in fact caught between the ending of that period of Loos, Hoffmann, and others, and the rise of a more dogmatic and established modernism. Our argument is that, if you have a calling that is "incompatible" with the seemingly established forces of the present, you have to continue doing what you think is right. And we say this because we see it today. There are groups of architects that actually suffer under the plight of a certain dogma, and they will never be recognized, Nicolás. They will never be heard of because it is not within the discourse of academics, for instance.

NDA   Is there something autobiographical about this assertion?

LN   You know, several people have brought up this question in relation to the show. I don't think it was our intention, but maybe there are parallels. After we went to Shanghai, it took us a bit longer than some of our peers to enter into the field of discourse and debate that academic institutions create. So, we'd question ourselves and the relevance of what we were

144

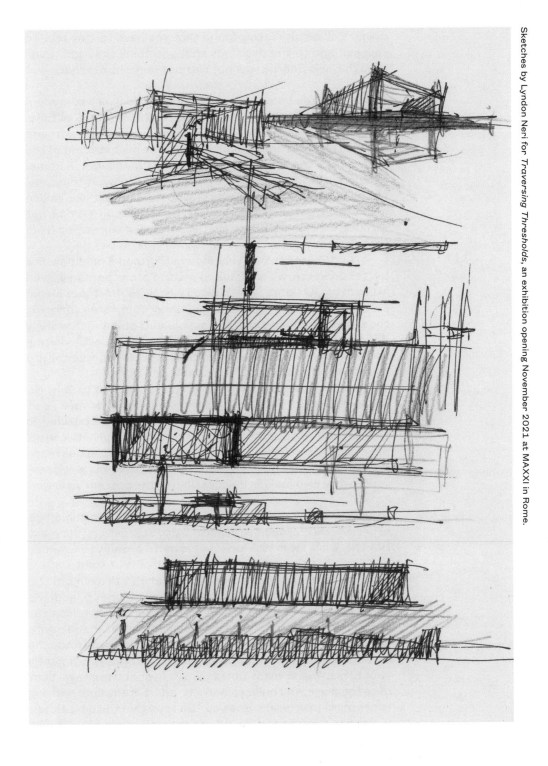

Sketches by Lyndon Neri for *Traversing Thresholds*, an exhibition opening November 2021 at MAXXI in Rome.

SKETCHES FOR A SCARPA SHOW

doing. But we ultimately found that you have to stay true to yourself and to the decisions that you think are right. Even though Carlo Scarpa was not without fault, he did that.

NDA   Absolutely. You know, I never considered Scarpa a bold architect, but now I find him very bold. I've read some of the lectures that he gave in the 1960s where he said something like, "I can't escape that I was the best student of the best student of the architect of the Monumento a Vittorio Emanuele II in Rome." No one would admit to being a part of that lineage at that time! I think accepting this as part of who he was, just like Venice might have also been a part of who he was, is quite simple but striking for the discourse that we are used to reading from that period.

     I find Scarpa to be a very interesting model right now. For better or worse, we are back to a world of the personal, even in teaching. As Jorge Silvetti discussed in his AIA Topaz Medallion lecture in 2018, personal pedagogy dominates curricula today and makes the idea of a school of thought increasingly difficult to foster in departments. The mania with visiting critics increasingly makes it so that schools represent little other than a diversity of fashionable positions.

     I think Scarpa is very attractive in relation to this. He is absolutely personal, but at the same time, deeper readings reveal more. There are relationships between what is biographical and historiographical in his work and between his obsessions and the way they intersected larger issues more broadly relevant to his time. I think this gives his work relevance while also making it accessible to the present situation.

LN   I agree. A lot of architects who come to work at our office, especially the Europeans, dismiss Carlo Scarpa very, very fast. But there is a lot in his work that is more broadly relevant to our discipline than what our eyes catch at first sight.

     The process that you see in Scarpa's drawing in the archive, of going over and over five or six schemes to address an issue, is something I appreciate immensely because our practice does it too. Scarpa obsessively goes over and over a very specific issue or condition in a project until he finds the solution that is just right for it. I think practice is ultimately about this. And so many times you try over and over again but miss the mark. You build something, and it is absolutely wrong in proportion or scale. But you still try again the next time.

     I find that process kind of interesting, and that's why today I'm looking closely at Valerio Olgiati's work and, to a certain extent, Peter Zumthor's. People don't understand

ENTRY,
PIVOT
NERI

SKETCHES FOR A SCARPA SHOW

Peter Zumthor, and they tag his work as highly personal. I think he's dismissed in academia and even among many of his Swiss peers. There is a kind of concerted effort to make him less relevant than he is. But what he does is really not easy, and it has great value beyond himself.

NDA It goes back to the fact that academia moves too fast through ideas, particularly as it becomes increasingly detached from a commitment to the practice of architecture. Practice forces you to evaluate architectural positions and strategies a bit more slowly and robustly, because you have to do it at the pace at which buildings allow. If we just think, draw and discuss, we miss that important step where we are forced to evaluate how our ideas fared when they confronted reality. It's easy for academics in the design curriculum that do not seriously practice to jump between new ideas every half decade and stay afloat in the attention economy. They are unencumbered by the act of building, and the evidence of the work they leave behind is much easier to forget when it begins to reveal cracks and wrinkles.

LN I want to show you an image here, let me turn this around. Do you see that photograph?

NDA Yes. Oh, it's …

LN That's Melnikov's house photographed by Candida Höfer. Doing work of that nature, being avant-garde—it's so easy today, I would argue. Yes, it's beautiful, and I love the work; the way he takes two circles and splits them to have an eye in the middle. I love the work, don't get me wrong; it's right here in our office. And I'm not saying that it was easy to do in its context. But that's one house that Melnikov was good at. All of the other work is less interesting. And there are a lot of these practices celebrated in academia like that nowadays, practices enjoying what I call their "Melnikov moment." There's definitely merit in a work like this, but we have to start questioning what value we assign to it as architects.

NDA That is precisely why Scarpa is interesting right now. The work is not so … intellectually loud. What attracts me to it now is precisely the fact that it isn't overly rhetorical. I think we are all pretty tired of the verboseness and excess of rhetoric that some of the less interesting postmodernists—Robert Venturi, for one—introduced into architectural discourse. But you see it even if you look at people like Aldo Rossi, how he

Sketches by Lyndon Neri for *Traversing Thresholds*, an exhibition opening November 2021 at MAXXI in Rome.

SKETCHES FOR A SCARPA SHOW

rewove architecture's relationship to the city and to history. There is a translation of his rhetorical thinking that comes into architecture too directly. Architecture is a completely different form of cultural expression than writing.

Scarpa feels a lot more accessible right now, maybe because his translation of ideas into buildings is more attuned to what buildings can actually communicate and do.

LN   Yes, interesting. I hear you. And don't get me wrong, it's also something we struggle with.

I just presented a project yesterday for a resort. The project is as commercial as commercial can be. And I got so lost in the conceptual rhetoric of the work I was showing that by the time the meeting was over, the client said, "Oh Lyndon, can we … give us two weeks to digest."

After the presentation Rossana told me, "Lyndon, you were in your own world in that presentation. You were in your own world. You have forgotten that you are designing for a client." Which was true.

I'm not saying we shouldn't continue to pursue what we are interested in—what will remain of purely disciplinary concern—but I think the good thing is the built work will force you to deal with what is of today and to reflect on how you can actually make a difference in this world with these interests.

Imagine if we didn't have the practice to tie us down. The bottom line is that if we don't deliver value to the world out there—to a client—we won't get paid. I think ultimately that's a reality that is often good for us as architects. It balances everything.

David Foster &
Zachary Mollica

with Kimberley
Huggins

Hemlock Rings and Tree Forks

On Common Ground

KIMBERLEY HUGGINS   Welcome, David and Zac!

ZACHARY MOLLICA   Thank you for having me. It is really exciting, but, David, I just hope that we don't encourage too many GSD students to come down to your forest and cause trouble.

DAVID FOSTER   Well, as I told Kimberley, there was once a tremendous amount of interaction between the GSD and the Harvard Forest. This was when I first arrived at Harvard, but other than our enduring connection with Professor Richard Forman, the relationship gradually withered away for a variety of reasons. It has been a real regret of mine to see it diminish.

ZM   Well, I take it back then.

KH   [*laughs*] We're all on the same page then. I would love to begin by giving you both space to share a bit about yourselves, your work, and the forest campuses you care for.

DF   Yes, it would be helpful for me to hear a bit about your forest, Zac.

ZM   The simplest explanation is that as part of the AA Design + Make program, we have 350 acres of forest named Hooke Park as our campus in Dorset, England. The forest is mixed-species, but in a very compartmentalized manner. It was actually clear-felled postwar and then replanted with species segregated into their own bounds of monospecies crops. At this point though, and interestingly for an architecture school, these timbers have grown enough to serve serious purposes in students' work.

     If someone was asked to guess which architecture school in the world had 350 acres of forest though, I don't think a single person would guess the Architectural Association school, and this makes for a really interesting twist. There is a strange mixture of technology and fantasy that comes together in our forest.

We pick up on a history of experimental architecture education that precedes our Design + Make program by about 30 years. Our predecessors at Hooke sought to demonstrate the potential of forest products that are deemed low-value from a commercial perspective. Their early buildings also now sit in the center of our campus. The design–build-oriented program set up by our director Martin Self continues to grow the campuses' infrastructure around these structures. The program is not unlike Rural Studio, but it has a more explicit brief that we remain in the forest full-time, that we use the materials we are surrounded by, and that we bring any computer and fabrication tools that we can to those pursuits.

Our primary focus is on the buildings that our students create, but increasingly there is also an interest in broadening the students' eyes to the ecological value of the site. Ultimately, the architects should develop a greater awareness of the timber they specify and understand how their choices influence the forests from which those trees come.

There is a history of connections running between the GSD and the Harvard Forest. Landscape architecture professors Carl Steinitz and Dana Tomlin once ran semester-long design studios and week-long pre-semester workshops in the Harvard Forest. Ecologists Mike Binford and Sharon Collinge were embedded within the GSD through Richard Forman, who then provided a bridge to the forest. Due to changes in administration over time, most connections to the forest were lost. Forman, however, still spends one day a week there.

KH   There is a mixture of academia and a sense of full presence in place that exists in both of your forests, but this combination is actually rare in formal education.

DF   Yes, the observation that we are both immersed in our forests is actually really important. The Harvard Forest is unusual that way. There are many schools that have ecological programs, and there are many schools that have field stations, but there are almost no other schools in the United States in which the field station is actually the department, the home for faculty and senior staff, and, as much as we can make it, the home for students.

Interestingly enough, the Harvard Forest was originally based in the business school in Cambridge. The founding members took a broad approach that involved economics and biology, and, later on, embraced design, art, and literature. In any case, soon after starting the forestry program, the dean decided that it needed to be immersed in the environment that it was actually operating with. Rather than having the students and faculty take forays from the city into the forest, they decided that they would move the school out into the landscape, and the director was sent off on a quest to evaluate potential sites.

154

Clearly, it needed to have a location that was relatively accessible to Cambridge. It also needed to be in an operating landscape, right? Accessible, but distant enough from the city that it was true to the rural environment. And, of course, it needed to encompass a large chunk of land that was still affordable. Eventually, they identified a site in Petersham. It is 65 miles west of Cambridge in a transition zone between southern New England and northern New England where there is this wonderful diversity of tree species.

I have come to believe that the dean's motivation to move was as much socially oriented as it was ecologically oriented. One of the great values of working here is that the vast majority of us live someplace in the regional landscape analogous to Petersham. We're immersed in the local communities and understand the challenges that come from rural life, from rural economies, from competition with the city, and from being avoided by the political and economic powers of the world. We understand the kind of ownerships and challenges that make managing the New England landscape so difficult.

So, they bought this forest. Any group today could find a bigger forest, maybe a better forest, or lots of comparable examples, but at this point, the one thing they couldn't buy is an understanding of a forest that is grounded in no less than a century's worth of intensive research. The first director recognized that the key to understanding the current landscape is through its history. As soon as he arrived in Petersham in 1907, he started assembling clues to the landscape's history. Now, we have a center with 110 years of research—both contemporary research data plus retrospective data going back 10,000 years. That is actually the true value of our forest.

KH   There are so many realities intersecting in forestry and you both are viewing them through different disciplinary lenses, but your forests share enough unique conditions, priorities, and methods that it might be fairly natural for you two to share in the accomplishments of the other.

It would have been great to walk through both of your forests today, but instead we will recreate that experience with the objects you brought. Zac, you brought these plates from the *Encyclopédie Méthodique de la Marine* with you. Could you tell us about them?

ZM   These images have become a keystone reference for advanced timber architecture. These are plates from an encyclopedia of wooden boat-building techniques, and they show that we can

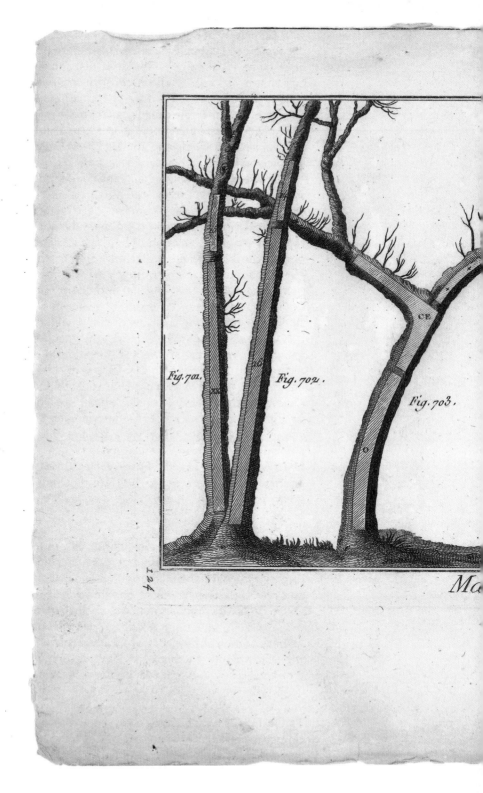

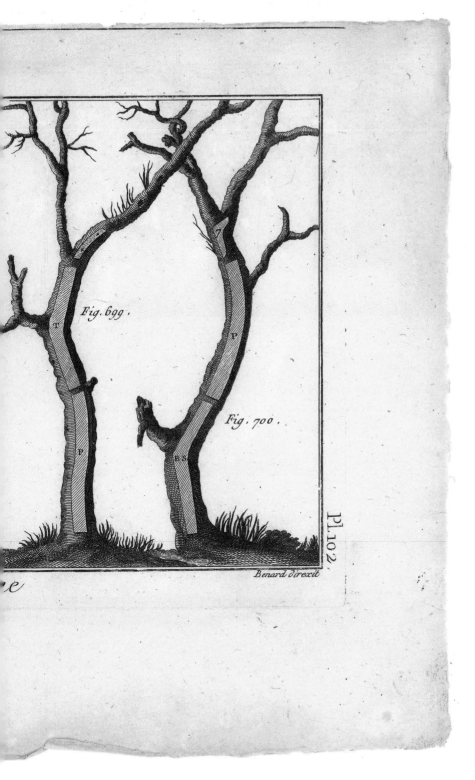

Fig. 699.

Fig. 700.

Pl. 102.

Benard direxit.

HEMLOCK RINGS AND TREE FORKS

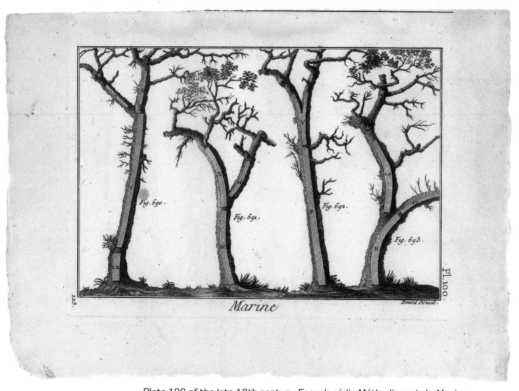

Plate 100 of the late 18th century *Encyclopédie Méthodique de la Marine*.

DAVID FOSTER & ZACHARY MOLLICA WITH KIMBERLEY HUGGINS

Plate 103 of the late 18th century *Encyclopédie Méthodique de la Marine.*

HEMLOCK RINGS AND TREE FORKS

read more potential shapes than straight lines in trees. We begin to understand from these drawings that branching trees once had extreme value and that tree species in our forest, like beech, which for the most part these days we are told are not desirable from a forestry perspective, might as well. Not only did nonlinear components have a potential use, but they were also fundamentally stronger than the alternatives.

It is this thinking that inspires the work at Hooke. In other words, can we reapproach the poorest reasoning of the industrial paradigm, seen in the use of the two-by-four, which seems to get worse every single year? Can we foster more creativity and use the diverse elements of the forest? There are ecological arguments in favor of this, but the key inspiration for us is that this approach might also allow for more advanced buildings. Our uses of timber have become dumb, quite simply. And while I think that we at Hooke can sometimes risk overcelebrating craftsmanship of the past, we are intentional in taking it as a starting point from which we bring in 3D scanning, robotics, and whatever else we may use.

DF   I love these images and that explanation. The move away from the dumbed down industrial and commercial thinking arises here as well, but what I really love about this image is that each of the trees displays a history in its form. Most of our forests won't produce trees like that anymore. You need particular growth conditions or human activities for trees to grow into those forms.

ZM   Now that you point them out, these forms have actually become an obsession of mine.

DF   You may be interested in this then. A couple of years ago, I finished a book on the history and biology of Martha's Vineyard island and observed that all the great tree forms that define this island are legacies of the past. The scattered individual trees that remain have a tremendous variety of shapes and forms as they have been affected by the wind, by grazing animals, and by the actions of people. Effectively, none of those conditions persist on the island today. These majestic trees are old relics of a past and are now gradually disappearing.

KH   Given this growth history, David—Zac, has Hooke's history made it difficult to actually find a variety of tree forms?

ZM   There are very few, and it gets right to the point that David is making. Due to a lack of management in the 30 years after

160

being planted, many trees became overcrowded and are now in this funny position where they haven't grown to be the tree that they were initially imagined to be. We would be hard-pressed to find four trees, as these images show, perfectly in a row that could help us, but if we walk the woods carefully and track tree GPS positions, then we can certainly find trees that speak to some of this complexity.

KH   If they are that rare, it must be difficult to know what to do once you've found them. Do you find yourself reading trees in general, like how the author of the encyclopedia plate is studying their forms?

ZM   Yes. In fact, even when I'm walking around Bedford Square in front of the AA, I find myself wanting to take a nice London planetree down! It has really taken years to get over the slightly jarring inability to look at a forked piece of timber and not just dream of cutting it down, which shouldn't be our only instinct.

KH   David, you also brought this image of a Hemlock cross section. I would love it if you could bring us a step further by reading something in the internal structure of a tree.

DF   This image happens to be a cross section of the oldest hemlock that Bob Marshall, founder of The Wilderness Society and a national advocate for forest and wildland protection, uncovered as he was doing a unique reconstruction of the forest's history in the 1920s for his master's degree at the Harvard Forest.
      His conclusions were grounded in this type of cross-sectional work where he interpreted the way that individual trees responded to an opening in the woods, whether it was generated by human activity or by natural processes, such as wind damage. His thesis begins in a very elegant way with this particular cross section and points out that the extremely dense rings at the core, seen next to the knife, actually predate the European colonization of North America, when this hemlock remained in the forest understory for a hundred years or so. The different types of growth episodes that followed were due, not to changes in the climate but to changes in the physical environment of the forest itself. The massive deforestation and extraction period of the mid-19th century removed the layer of trees that this hemlock had been growing underneath and led to a rapid increase in growth rate as seen in the significantly thicker ring depositions and cracks along the radii.

The aim of his thesis was very practical and asked, "How would we control the relative abundance of hemlocks versus white pine growing on this particular site?" Ultimately, he sought to advise on commercial forestry practices and went on to become an illustrious thinker and actor in conservation, forestry, and ecology.

KH   This cross-sectional work is a great example of a kind of experimental analog work that is still very present in the Harvard Forest today. But over the past hundred years, there has also been a natural layering of increasingly advanced technologies. How do those two realities coexist within the Harvard Forest?

DF   We combine old-fashioned, pedestrian approaches to characterizing the forest—laying out immense plots on the ground where we locate and measure each tree's dimensions—with handheld and aerial mapping to capture the actual three-dimensional form of the forest. The ground-based measurements are used to verify that the LiDAR reconstructions are accurate. There are fabulous images that come out of that. Some are at the cutting edge of assessing the amount of carbon in the forest or the interactions among trees.

The Harvard Forest was one of the first places to do intensive work in the 1940s and 1950s with aerial photography, an image technology that came out of wartime. This is just a continuation of that, but it's because we have these pedestrian tracts in which every tree has been measured and mapped that all these people with new technologies are attracted to the site for testing. Each person then attracts additional people. It has an "if you build it, they will come"-type of cascading effect.

KH   I wonder if Hooke has been successful in incorporating advanced technologies for similar reasons. 3D scanning processes and tools are a regular feature in your work and the work of your students, Zac, but in a way that is integrated with traditional building methods. What has your experience been threading between the two?

ZM   First, I'll simply say that David is right: the imagery that comes through is magical. You're treated to these impossible views, and the joy of this imagery lies in the closeness that you feel to the woods. In applying it to our design work, 3D scanning individual pieces of wood has become an incredible platform that allows us to use the wood's natural shape in some way.

162

The first instance of incorporating scanning into the program was in fact close to reenacting the process of old ship-builders. Students surveyed the forest with a small template, held it against a tree and said, "Yes, we estimate that's about right." Roughly 200 trees were cataloged this way before scanning. There are efforts to expand our scanning capability because there is a risk that our projects are entirely relevant if you have a 350-acre forest, a skilled forester, and a workshop manager who is actually a mad genius-inventor-engineer. The risk is that we create these projects that are incredible and evocative but can't be replicated.

In recent years, our forester and a new robotics developer have pushed the scale of scanning, and now we are imagining what a design program could do with a scan of the whole forest. A student might be able to say, "I'm after a piece of timber that's about this," and the program might say, "Well, that's just over there." It encourages another way of seeing the forest.

Even in this use of trees though, we're only making decisions based on their external shape and assuming that this is enough to know. Thinking of the hemlock cross section that David spoke about, I'm still struck by how little we engage the complexities of trees and then, as well, our burning need to use them. We use wood as a much simpler material than it truly is.

KH   You touched on the increasing focus on wood construction and engineered wood materials that is occurring within, as you described earlier, still very simple industrial and standardized frameworks. Looking at the Wood Chip Barn project—an insane project in the best way—what lessons did this project impart to you and your collaborators that might be helpful as the design field moves toward wood?

ZM   Having engaged in it as a student where you are in over your head, working hours beyond what's real or reasonable, it took those of us leading the project as students maybe six months after completion to understand what we had done. As far as we were concerned at the time, we were just doing something crazy to learn a lot of things in the forest.

The direct answer is that probably nobody should ever build exactly what we built again; the project is riddled with problems. The truly important thing is that it opens a way of thinking with timber that I hope is infectious, and I hope anyone interested learns from the techniques used.

Emanuel Jannasch from Dalhousie uses the term "hyper-industrial" to describe our approach as a society. There's

163

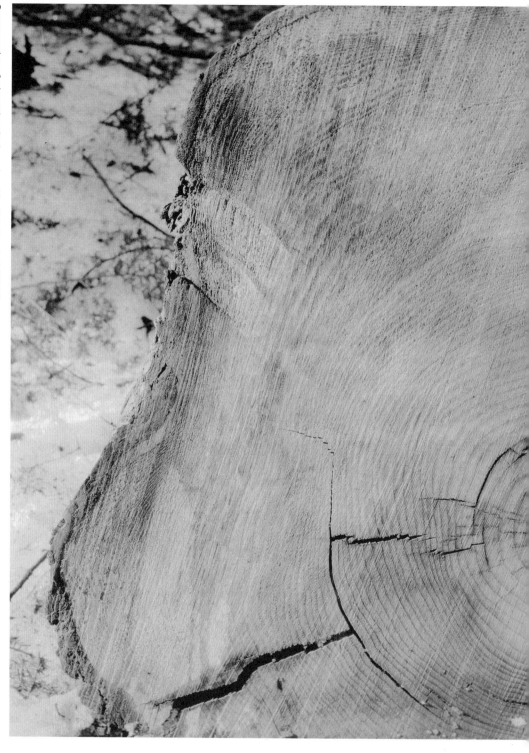

Cross section of a large hemlock analyzed by Bob Marshall (1924).

DAVID FOSTER & ZACHARY MOLLICA WITH KIMBERLEY HUGGINS

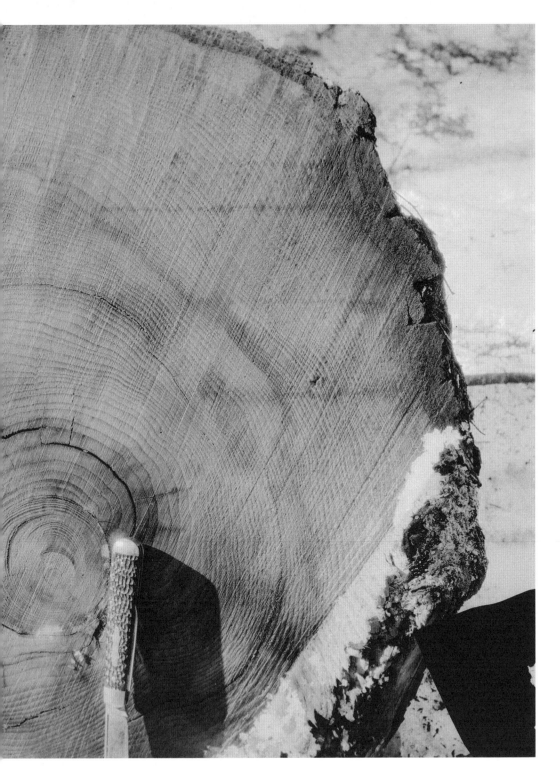

165 HEMLOCK RINGS AND TREE FORKS

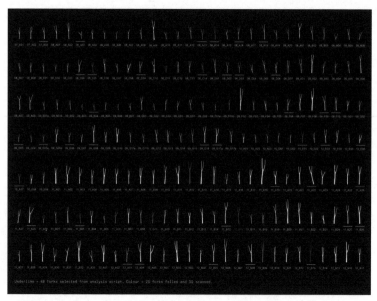

Database of 204 Beech forks surveyed as potential elements for the truss.

a belief that by pivoting to CLT [cross-laminated timber], we're going to save the world through building and that more timber used is inherently better, but what this misses is the true potential of digital tools. It feels like we're applying digital tools to do exactly what we've done through the entire Industrial Revolution, which is to further process and standardize. The hope here is to say that it might be better to use these tools to dance very gently around a material which is already complex. Architects are building things to be formally complex, and yet to get there, we first cut things into squares, bend them, glue them, cut away from them, and then hopefully find a use for that sawdust.

To build in the way we did was an utterly collaborative effort among probably 10 different disciplines, with forestry being chief among them. What was fundamental to this project, and hopefully will be more broadly fundamental, is engagement at every part along that stream. You need good and confident engineers if you're going to attempt these projects, because the reality is that there is no established method.

KH   And what was it like to work without an established method?

ZM   Well, in this photo of the truss being preassembled, one of us is about to hit this precisely fabricated structure with a sledgehammer while ratchet straps pull it in three different directions, hoping that everything is going to kind of slip into place [*laughs*]. To me, there is a lovely absurdity to the project, which is to say we used a robot capable of repeatedly cutting something to within a thousandth of a millimeter, and yet the beech was felled maybe a month previous and was still green enough that it was moving millimeters each day as it dried. You wonder whether that makes any sense or if it might actually be a good thing that a digital process doesn't become a fully digital process. It leaves room for human interaction and care.

The project is an exciting start to an idea that has shattered and splintered into about 12 to 20 smaller projects where others look at the same ideas differently: looking to the crown, looking to the root plate under the ground, and looking to understand how you might design something to pick up on the growth of trees.

DF   That is a much more elegant and elaborated characterization of something going on all around us here as well. Today, I actually had to skip a meeting on a long-term dialogue on developing more CLT manufacturing capability and applications to join this conversation.

The application of really cutting-edge technology to better utilize the raw material is so interesting to think about. There's so little effort moving in that direction. It's all moving toward standardization, industrialization, reductionism; take our trees and turn them into something that can then make these standard materials. CLT is a marvelous material, and marvelous buildings can be made with it, but it can also drive a lot of terrible activity in the woods and affect the ways in which we connect nature with our lives. So this is marvelous to see.

ZM   Thank you, David.

KH   I'd be curious to know what the conversations surrounding increased wood and CLT application are like from the conservation side of things, David. Would you tell us a bit about the "Wildlands and Woodlands" vision that you and your colleagues are working to bring forward in New England?

DF   There are actually some interesting connections and threads to what we were just talking about. To begin, you have to look at this graph here, which clearly shows the trends of deforestation and reforestation. You just can't help but think, "What a phenomenal dynamic." If we look at the forest during the lifetime of somebody like Henry David Thoreau in the middle of the 19th century, we see it is on one trajectory: downward.

The transportation of selected Beech forks for 3D scanning.

The period of clearing and extracting resources was so intense that Thoreau fully expected all the forests of New England to disappear in his lifetime.

The New England landscape holds this incredible story of resilience, but coming up on the 21st century, we noticed rather suddenly that the forests are declining again. As scientists, we knew a different future had to be possible, but who was defining that future? A group of academic ecologists and conservationists at the Harvard Forest and across New England decided to write a paper that essentially said, "Having recovered this wonderful forest, we have a second opportunity to determine the fate of our forested landscape. Let's do it differently this time. Let's conserve that forest." We were absolutely dumbfounded when conservation groups, state agencies, and other people said, "Well, that's a marvelous vision! How are you—and we—going to do it?"

So, that is what we've been spending all of our time on since 2005. How do you accomplish the stabilization of our forest cover, the stabilization of our agricultural cover, while building our communities? That is the "Wildlands and Woodlands" vision. If we did nothing more to the New England landscape in terms of human activity, it would still change in major ways for the next few centuries because the whole system is still recovering from the intensive historical use since European arrival. To maintain the full diversity there, we have to

DAVID FOSTER & ZACHARY MOLLICA WITH KIMBERLEY HUGGINS

The preassembly of robotically-fabricated truss elements before being erected on site.

maintain some of these cultural landscapes in order to be productive and continue to support the plants and animals that are dependent on them.

We also hope to continue the rewilding. All of the major animals that were missing from Henry David Thoreau's landscape are back with the exception of wolves and cougars. He would never have guessed that there would be moose or bear at Walden Pond. In his day, the single largest native mammal was the muskrat. Now, we have deer, beavers, coyotes, wild turkeys, peregrine falcons, and more. We want to encourage that, but we also want to retain the grasp on the birds and insects of young forests and grasslands. That requires balancing the wild, the managed, and the cultural.

KH   It seems like a large share of the effort lies in creating relationships between actors that might not have communicated otherwise: farmers, loggers, conservation groups, local communities, local governments, schools ...

DF   Yes, and I should say that the American ethic in conservation is largely one that only embraces the wild and the natural. The appreciation for cultural landscapes, traditional practices, and their value in land management may be natural to you, Kimberley, even obvious, but it doesn't have a terribly strong foundation in forestry, ecological thinking, or even

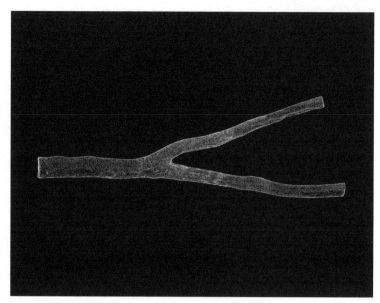
A detailed 3D scan to be computationally arranged into a truss structure.

conservation planning in most of the United States. I only became aware of it after the time I spent researching in Scandinavia or with individuals like Oliver Rackham and imported it from Northwestern Europe into my work. This appreciation seeks to recognize, respect, and embrace the fact that people have a millennial history of shaping landscapes and to incorporate that understanding into modern conservation and land management.

A lot of what we're trying to encourage is exactly analogous to the application of new technology to traditional materials and treatment of the land. While culturally and historically-inspired land management is an approach that is advancing on many different fronts, it is still just a shadow to the commercial, industrial, and mechanized approaches that are rampant across the landscape.

KH In the spirit of incorporating a form of appreciation that's not typical to your field, what about Hooke Park? Is there any consideration to supporting wildlife in the campus masterplan and harvesting program?

ZM Sure. I actually jumped to this call from a beaver webinar that I joined with our forester. It's an incredibly complex part of being in the UK. Fundamentally, those processes started much earlier and have been done much more thoroughly to remove

The beech fork truss after construction. The figure pictured on the left is Zachary Mollica.

every species. An interesting part of being a Canadian here is the realization that Hooke Park is a very strange forest because it feels as much like a park—and park is in the name—as it does a wild forest. I can go for a run with headphones on and not fear anything more than a pheasant scaring me.

We certainly have diverse bird species in the woods and a population of deer, but there is absolutely a disparity. Larger fauna just aren't really there. I think we're guilty of not paying enough attention to wildlife, and I'm not implicating our forester who does pay attention to it, but I think he needs more support in that. It's been exciting recently to see energy arise across the country for the reintroduction of species, even just in starting with keeping Canadians like me happy by bringing in beavers.

KH   It is striking to think about how long it can take these systems to recover. Has uncovering the history of a landscape that has experienced catastrophic changes—something evident in the material you've spoken about today, David—given you perspective on our current crisis?

DF   With all of the stress from climate, disease, and exotic-insect outbreaks, it remains true that the largest threat to our eastern forests is direct human impact: overly intensive harvesting of forests in Maine and northern New England and

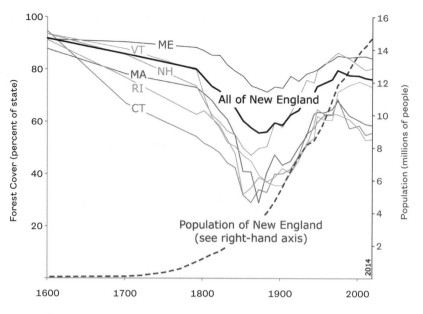

The decline and recovery of the New England forest, beginning with an indigenous population of roughly 75–100 thousand people through to our present moment.

deforestation for everything from buildings to roads, energy transmission, and solar production. These forests are remarkably resilient if we will leave them alone, but they cannot recover from being replaced by hard surfaces. It remains to be seen whether and how they will regrow up north if we give them a chance.

KH   What might the responsibilities of designers be in order to operate with, rather than against, an effort like the "Wildlands and Woodlands"?

DF   "Designers." What do you mean by that?

KH   Oh. That's a fair question. I'm coming from landscape architecture, where the overlap with ecology is perhaps the most inseparable compared to disciplines like architecture or urban design, but the desire to shape the built environment responsibly is shared. Even so, unless you are someone with Zac's experience, encompassing growing, harvesting, fabricating, and building into a design process, which is rare, most design work exists within a reality disengaged from the people and landscapes that produce our materials and from the wildlife dependent on it all. It's hard to know how to contribute.

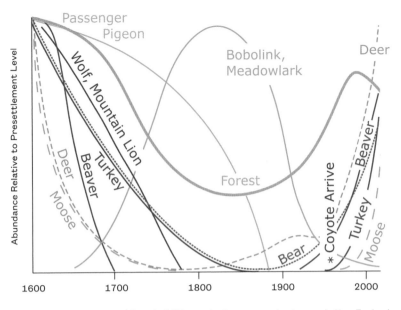

The changing composition of wildlife species in response to changes in New England forest cover.

DF   I mean, at so many different scales that is absolutely critical and yet something that there isn't really any interface for. I come from the field of ecology, and what we're advancing would be known as "land conservation." What's fascinating is that there is very little interface between the two worlds.

Conservation proceeds as a means of conserving the land and finding legal ways of protecting it that are outside of the world of planning and regulation, but those obviously, obviously need to be completely integrated and mutually supportive. In terms of this, the question is, "Why aren't there more people with Zac's knowledge and approach?" The biggest criticism of the Graduate School of Design made by those I know who teach there has always been that the students don't actually have any practical knowledge of the natural world, right? For example, Mike Binford, Peter del Tredici, or Betsy Colburn teach a very basic understanding of ecosystems, but that's because it's completely missing otherwise. The students do all their design thinking and work without that kind of connection. They can't identify trees, let alone dissect them, and think about their internal structure and the properties within them.

So, we don't have very much common ground.

KH   What would it take to find common ground?

DF   You need motivation, and you need translators, right?

KH   Right.

DF   We need people who cross those boundaries. Neither world has the motivation, and we don't have many people sitting in the center who can forge those connections.

      You have to have the right people in the right places, but those connections may or may not be there at any given department or school.

KH   Who is someone from the forest's history who exemplified that ability?

DF   Someone like Bob Marshall was distinctive in that way. His work was very practical—"How do we manage forests to achieve a particular result?"—but his passion in life was wilderness. He wanted to preserve raw nature in an industrialized world that was getting further and further from nature. He realized that the only way that he was going to achieve a high enough position of leadership to exert influence on a national entity like the US Forest Service would be if he acquired the practical skills to actually know how to manage forests well. He had to know an awful lot more than just what raw nature is all about.

      So, he didn't become an ecologist, he became a forester and developed a position of authority. From that position, he was able to create the Wilderness Society, which has gone on to be a great leader in things like the Wilderness Act and the preservation of all these great lands that we have.

      In there, there's this link between forestry and ecology and between practical use and the understanding of nature, the kind of linkages that I think you're after.

KH   Zac, what would you say has driven the individuals in Hooke's lineage?

ZM   I think the one thing that ties everyone at Hooke together is a beguilement with trees, which is an interesting aspect to underline. Where I get frustrated with discussions similar to the one David mentioned not joining today is that my interest in timber has nothing to do with its sustainable credibility. Weird thing to say, but in a way that's just a bonus. Really, I think approaching timber as a box to check in order to certify a building as or to make a building more "green" is usually

174

accepting a false premise at the starting point. For a lot of us here, it's simply an obsession with this material that has a full life.

It has been a time of marked change for Hooke recently. In the past five years or so, Frei Otto, Ted Happold, Ted Cullinan, and Richard Burton—all central figures—have passed away. Yet their buildings within the campus endure and become our teachers in a way. We used to spend an hour every day eating lunch in the Prototype House and typically you'd spend most of that time looking up at the rafters, having finished your food, thinking about who was up there.

We're only getting started and we are doing some good projects, but I also know how much more could be done. One great thing I hope comes from this conversation, Kimberley, is to say that I'd love to pull David into conversations with our students and staff, because there are not enough schools or forests being used in the right ways. I feel like there are connections that we can bring forward.

DF   Yeah, that was great of Kimberley to bring us together.

KH   I'm grateful that you both could make time for and were open to this meeting. I'm sorry to have pulled both of you away from other discussions though. The CLT dialogue and also the … well, the beaver conversation.

ZM   [laughs]

DF   [laughs] I'd much rather be in the beaver conversation— let me tell you!

Sumayya Vally

with Vladimir Gintoff

Islamic Heritage Project

On Language and Meaning

VLADIMIR GINTOFF   You formed Counterspace with fellow students while you were still studying at the University of the Witwatersrand. How would you like to change pedagogy both in practice and as an educator yourself?

SUMAYYA VALLY   Counterspace has evolved several times in its very short lifespan, and I think that is largely due to the nature of collaboration with different disciplines and entities. Even our studio setup, which we call Counterparts, incorporates other practices into one space. Whether we're partnering with choreographers, performers, fashion designers, or anyone else, we never work in a supply-and-receive capacity, it's always a collaboration. And by working in proximity, we start to inform one another and speak similar languages, which is hugely beneficial.

   The studio formed as a response to a lack that we felt in the profession. As a student, I was incredibly enthused about and inspired by Joburg. We would often drive to different places in the city, walking and exploring the underbellies and working to learn them. I became concerned that after my time in school, where we had created this space of embodied research—walking through and experiencing the city—that I was going to end up in practice, in an office job, and become jaded, and that this desire to work in relation to the city would be numbed. When we formed the practice, for me, it was about perpetuating a sense of optimism and furthering a desire to understand and read our context, and to imagine and produce worlds suggested by and already living inside of it.

   Pedagogy offered a way to think longer and deeper on questions that can't be answered in the short space of a practice project. I was very lucky because I met Lesley Lokko, who founded the Graduate School of Architecture at the University of Johannesburg. At my graduation exhibition, when she saw

SUMAYYA VALLY WITH VLADIMIR GINTOFF

my work, she said, "Come and work with me." I had no idea who she was or what she was asking, but I said yes, and that really opened me up to pedagogy that can actually look different and be anything. Lesley's project was about creating a curriculum, specifically for the African continent, and my interests fit very naturally into that construction. Both pedagogy and practice enable new questions, and Lesley created a generous environment for working without focusing on outcomes.

VG   Your Unit 12 studio course at the Graduate School of Architecture seeks to create a uniquely African architectural vocabulary, a "Contemporary African Almanac of Architectural Speculation." Could you discuss the ambition of creating cross-world spaces and how the Arabic term *hijra* aligns with these goals?

SV   The course has been going on for five years! The primary focus and beginnings of the studio were very much about finding form for things that are in flux. It embraces premises that come across as counterproductive or counterintuitive because architecture is so much about things that do not shift and that need to endure. In that way, the studio is not so focused on buildings, but on students bringing their own identities, perspectives, and lenses, and then on us trying to work through a relevant form of representation for that particular interest. But we also do have projects, and they can encompass land-, sea-, air-, and cyberscapes. Students have focused on edges, trade relations, cultural exchanges, crossings, mechanisms for control of species, objects, and conditions. Their work has been situated between many dualities, such as past and present, home and away, and through different ways of contextualizing these concepts. The challenge for students is to tell their own stories and to find the appropriate tools for representation. The real goal is to speculate with ambition and aplomb on how to select form, structure, materials, and programs for a uniquely African architectural vocabulary, or what we call a "Contemporary African Almanac of Architectural Speculation."

The term *hijra* has many meanings: "immigrating," "passing," or "coming," and interestingly, it has both Latin and Arabic roots. Historically, it described the Prophet Muhammad's flight from Mecca to Medina to escape persecution. The etymology includes the words for "departure," "exodus," and "journey." In Urdu, the term has also come to mean "fluidity of identity" or a third identity for gender and culture. The

ISLAMIC HERITAGE PROJECT

body is understood to be a literal site of transition, a vessel through which culture and identity journey, a place in which both are housed.

Traditionally, the role of architecture has allowed for the confining or controlling of space, shaping historical experience and social relations through a static form. As a result, the history of peoples, for whom movement, not stasis, is the predominant experience, does not easily or directly translate into built form. The Unit 12 course is interested in finding strategies for the material and spatial representation of contemporary experience. Working with the students, we perceive enormous architectural potential in the migratory, the diasporic, the mythical, the performative, and the narrative, and seek to create new spatial possibilities for these themes.

VG   You have described Johannesburg as its own laboratory for speculative histories, futures, and new design languages. What makes the city so meaningful for you and your practice?

SV   The city has a very special energy in that everyone here is hustling and trying to make it in some kind of way. It's a city that's always been synonymous with migration and with movement from its inception as "The City of Gold." There's so much here in every direction, in all of the city's cracks, and it's inspiring to see how it functions both formally and informally. What I mean is that there are rogue economies and informal strategies for individuals and groups who are excluded or marginalized from the visible economy. People become industrious when they need to secure basic needs, such as transportation, living conditions, or practicing their beliefs.

It's easy to be romantic about it, especially as an architect. We often step back and say that we need to respect these practices, to only listen and let these things play out as they do. I agree with that somewhat, but I also think that it requires our agency and is our responsibility to engage with and respond to existing conditions and to develop them further.

VG   How do these ideas of engagement relate to your vision for this year's Serpentine Pavilion?

SV   I am deeply honored and also emboldened by this commission, that they chose this scheme, which is about reaching other voices, about collaboration and co-production with communities, and creating tentacles in other places. I think that

180

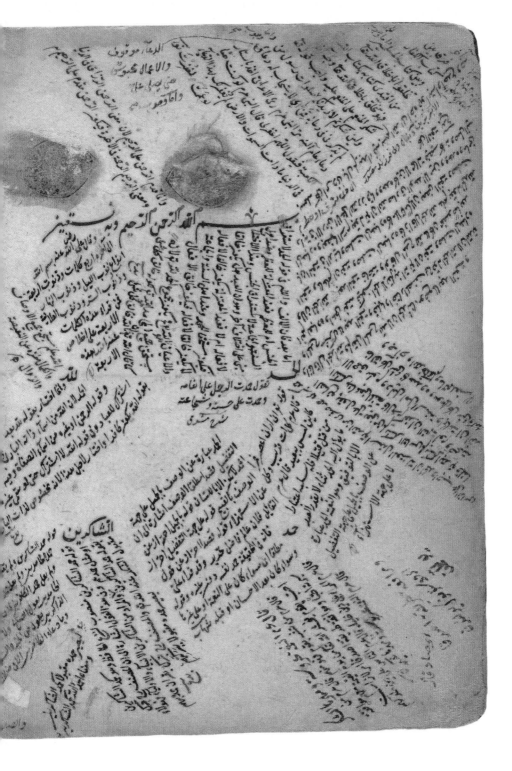

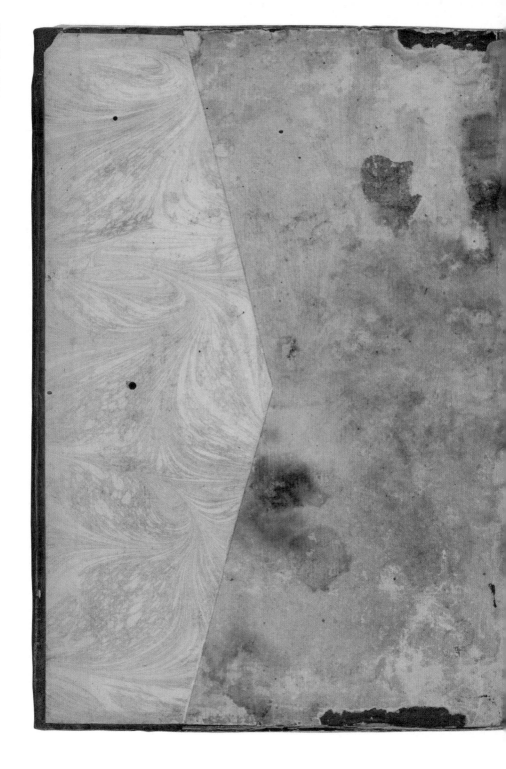

Title: Kitāb Talkhīṣ min mīzān al-kalimāt al-jafriyah wa-ḥawādith al-sinīn al-hijriyahi; al-Durr al-munazzam fī sharḥ al-ism al-aʿẓam. Date: unknown. Origin: unknown. Extent: 4 leaves, bound: 21 cm. Subject: Divination, Islamic Occultism. Language: Arabic. Courtesy of Islamic Heritage Project, MS Arab 374. Houghton Library, Harvard University.

SUMAYYA VALLY WITH VLADIMIR GINTOFF

it's important to remember that this commission happened before the rupture that the Black Lives Matter resurgence commanded last year, which of course, should always be on the agenda, but the moment forced other institutions to awaken and feel the need to respond.

I am moved that the Serpentine chose this commission before that moment and that they really used the extended time to listen deeply. I'm also pleased that this moment has happened, and I'm aware that on the one hand, as people of color, we are being called to respond much more and need to question levels of performativity and so on. On the other, it's also a moment for us to say something, and we need to be able to use it in the best way possible.

VG   We've seen that a global approach to design, like modernism, doesn't work as expected, but simultaneously, small-scale interventions can be stifled by their own restrictive scope. I wonder if you see the Serpentine Pavilion's engagement with the larger city of London through satellite pavilions as a way of creating a middle-scale for the discipline?

SV   Through this Pavilion's strategy of taking existing architectural fragments and piecing them together, we as designers are able to say new things. The process can lead someone experiencing the structure or its satellites down a path that they might not have noticed or recognized before. By practicing at various scales and paces simultaneously, we are able to ask different questions and see design problems through a different set of lenses. Are there more vibrant ways to define location rather than the physical site or scale alone? Can we become more agile and fluid in our understanding? The pavilion fragments are contextually linked by their locations and the audiences that experience them in those places. They reference other contexts and geographies of migration, even other time periods, and they draw on and honor typologies, such as acoustic architecture, calypsos, minbars, mihrabs, porch steps, stage sets, street iftars, market stalls, and other typologies of belonging.

VG   You created a work for the Serpentine as part of their *do it* series, which was revived recently. It's an old project where artists were chosen to create actions or instructions that would engage the general public. Yours was to reach out to someone old and have them convey a story, song, or recipe in their mother tongue. This got me thinking a lot about textiles

ISLAMIC HERITAGE PROJECT

and how they often come from multigenerational practices of knowledge sharing. What are your own connections to and feelings about craft? I mean that both in the literal sense of craft as making and in terms of how craft could and should be incorporated more into architecture.

SV   I don't think about it often, though I do have a deep connection to textiles because I'm from a family of migrants. My grandfather came to South Africa alone when he was six years old. A bit later, when he was a teenager, he started working and had a trade stall that then grew into stores and eventually to wholesale and so on, but always in textiles. At the start, it was very much focused on Basotho blankets, and when I was young we would visit textile factories and the villages connected to the practice.

These experiences are embedded in my thinking. And I'm in love with textiles. I am really interested in how so many of these crafts that we have in our context have not been absorbed. We have yet to draw out enough inspiration from them in terms of what they can do for architecture.

I think from that perspective the material politics of bringing in craft is also really, really important. I worked on an experimental project where we looked at integrating sugarcane husks into the work, which became a way to talk about difficult material histories. It was a means to think through concepts like plantations and labor and how to physically work them into a project. I'm now even thinking of hair braiding in Johannesburg and all the mathematics and patterns embedded in those practices. There is just so much that we can draw on in terms of design languages, and we just aren't doing it.

Returning to the *do it* project that you mentioned, which revolved around building an embodied archive of orations in mother tongues, I reached out to two people, and one of them was Yasmeen Lari. In our past project together, we worked with research on bamboo, lime, and mud structures, but I also got to meet and work with many of the women that she has trained to produce Kashi tiles and other crafts in Pakistan. Yasmeen and I talked a lot about how old methods and technologies can be translated into something that is contemporary. I think so much of this archive is disappearing and bringing these concepts into our practice is a way to honor them and to translate and visualize them as well.

VG   On the subject of stories and the preservation of ideas through text, I'd like for us to discuss Harvard's Islamic Heritage Project (IHP) and specifically a digital collection of scanned

الكراس الخامس

الكراس السادس

لقد كان حد السكر من قبل صلبه خفيف الذي اذ كان في شرع عنا جلدا
فلما بلغ المصلوب قتل صاحبي الا انه فان للحد تدجاوز للحدا

ثم دخلت سنة ٦٦٦ فيها توجه السلطان الى نحو البلاد الشامية وحاصر مدينة يافاه والشقيف وفتحهما ثم توجه الى انطاكية كبيرة فتحها ثم توجه الى بغراص فتحها ثم رجع الى مصر فزينت له ومدة وكان يوم دخوله يوما مشهودا ثم دخلت سنة ٦٦٦ فيها حج السلطان الى بيت الله الحرام وكان الوقف بالجمعة ثم رجع الى مصر وبعد ذلك شرع في ترتيب خيل البريد بسبب سرعة الاخبار اليها ثابتة وكانت الاخبار ترد عليه في الجمعة مرتين واصرف على جملة من المال لحق تم لذلك الترتيب ثم دخلت سنة ٦٦٧ فيها وردت الاخبار

بان اتغا ابن هلاكو ملك التتار قد ركب على البلاد الشامية وصل عسكره الى الفرات وصلوا البيرة فخرج اليهم السلطان ومعه سائر الامراء وكان جاليش العسكر ايبك الافرم الاتابكي ولايد يبسري فتلا شيا على الفرات فكان بينهما وقعة عظيمة وقتل من الفريقين ما لا يحصى وعدم رسم فلما دخل التتار الى البيرة اخلع على نائبها وبعاه على حاله وفرق شيا على من بها من العساكر لكل مقاتل ما يزيد بشار لانهم قاتلوا مع التتار قتال الموت حتى كسروهم فاقام السلطان في البيرة اياما ثم رجع الى حلب ثم توجه الى الشام ثم توجه الى القاهرة وكان يوم دخوله يوما مشهودا وحملت على رأس العبد والطير وزينت له القاهرة ثم دخلت سنة ٦٦٧

فيها وقع الطاعون بمصر وما ت من الناس ما لا يحصى من رجال ونسا واطفال وعبيد وجوار واقام نحو سنة اشهر وفيها كان النيل شحيحا وابطاعت ميعاد الوفا الى ايام الصيف وبلغ منتهى الزيادة ١٦ ذراعا و ١٧ قيراطا ثم هبط فوقع الغلا العظيم وحصل للناس من الضرر ما لا مزيد عليه بسبب ذلك فانا سرنا الى البرنا البحرة

ثم دخلت سنة ٦٦٧ فيها ارسل السلطان جش يده الى بلاد النوبة وسببه ان ملك النوبة دخل الى اسوان ونهب ما فيها واخرقها فلما بلغ السلطان ذلك عين لها العسكر فطلا وصلوا الى النوبة ورم الامرا والعساكر السلطان تقاتلوا مع ملك ما على اسوان نكرره اشد كسرة وقتلوا من عسكره ما لا يحصى وعا سروا اخوه واولاده واقاربه وغنموا منهم غنايم كثيرة من عبيد وجوار وخيول وغير ذلك ثم رجعوا الى مصر في غاية النصر

ثم دخلت سنة ٦٧٥ في ٢٢ من رجب الاولى توفي الى رحمة الله تعالى سيدي احمد البدوي النبوي والقرين العلوي سيدي احمد البدوي وكي اعاد اسر علينا من بركاته امين

Muraqqa'āt; album of Islamic calligraphy; album of Persian calligraphy. Date: unknown. Place of Origin: unknown. Extent: 1 v. (24 leaves); 34 cm. Description: 23 calligraphic compositions. Language: Persian. Courtesy of Islamic Heritage Project, MS Persian 34, Houghton Library, Harvard University.

SUMAYYA VALLY WITH VLADIMIR GINTOFF

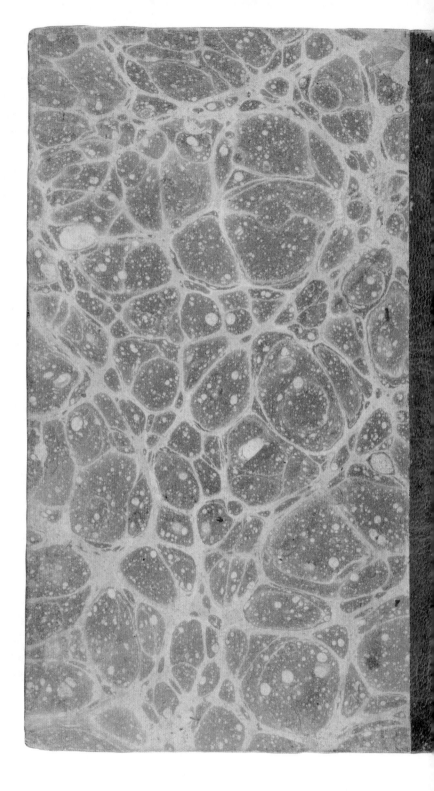

SUMAYYA VALLY WITH VLADIMIR GINTOFF

manuscripts, maps, and other texts found in the university's collections that span from the 10th to 20th centuries. I'm especially interested in the fact that a majority of the cataloged objects have no known provenance. Could you discuss how resources like the IHP archive, in its cataloging of historic forms of knowledge through handwriting and bookmaking, can be useful to design practice?

SV   Exemplified by the *do it* project, I'm interested in forms of embodied archives, in traditions that are carried in the body through tongues, breath, and bone. In Islamic tradition, the concept of *muttasil* refers to a continuous chain of narration in which each narrator has heard that narration from his or her teacher; knowledge being passed down directly from person to person, orally and through memory.

The Arabic word *mushaf* means "codex" or "collection of sheets," but it is also a concept that refers to a written copy of the Quran. This practice came about later in Islam, and so the tradition of preserving the entire Quran in the body through memory is still alive and present across the world. The body itself is an archive of language, sounds, genes, and health or other factors that cannot be easily catalogued or characterized through our now dominant forms of archiving.

I am intrigued by the ambiguity or difficulty of characterization in the Islamic Heritage Project for this reason. Even though these are written texts, the lack of knowledge available about their location of origin is a refusal to be categorized. It tells us that origins can be in several places, which speaks to histories of movement and entanglement and of bodies of knowledge. This interests me deeply.

VG   Texts have also allowed for particular languages to be preserved even as they have fallen out of favor in everyday parlance. I believe there are Qurans that have been made in South Africa employing Arabicized forms of Afrikaans that exist nowhere else in the world. How do these highly specific acts of cultural preservation and modes of distribution in your immediate context factor into your role as a designer with a global reach?

SV   The first time that Afrikaans was written down was by Cape Malay slaves in South Africa who had memorized the Quran and started to pen down transliterations in Arabicized Afrikaans. Again, this is interesting to me because it points to an entanglement of cultures, and the text embodies movement and flux in its form, bringing together territories through accent, annunciation, and *tajweed*, a common term in the context of Quran recitation. It comes from the Arabic word *jawada*, which linguistically means "enhancement" or making something outstanding.

I have also recently been working on research around the various melodies and traditions of the recitation of the *adhan*, which is the call to prayer or literally "to listen" in Arabic. Some of the research suggests that much of jazz and the blues were influenced by Africans who were travelling back from the Hajj pilgrimage and were captured as slaves and taken to the Americas. Again, these ideas held in spoken word, melody, and memory suggest archives that are dynamic and that resist categorization because of their hybridities.

VG   How do historic examples or episodes of hybridity factor into an African identity today? Are the various perspectives, shaped by centuries of influence by empire, colonialism, and migration, able to coexist in a unified approach or strategy for architecture?

SV   All of our identities are hybrid, and to perceive any identity as essentialist or "pure" is a falsehood. Many perspectives are shaped by colonialism, but each empire also borrowed and was affected by so many traditions and forms of knowledge. Nothing is ever as unified as we imagine. Hybridity shows how things can function in different contexts. So, rather than focus on reasserting the validity of certain traditions, I operate with an implicit embrace of richness, diversity, and levels of depth and texture. We all need to be able to honor and find ways of seeing and listening to what is already here in our contexts and how practices can manifest into forms or create new ones.

Architecture is behind in terms of its lexicon. If we derived or incorporated more from other worldviews and vocabularies, the practice would be much richer and more complex.

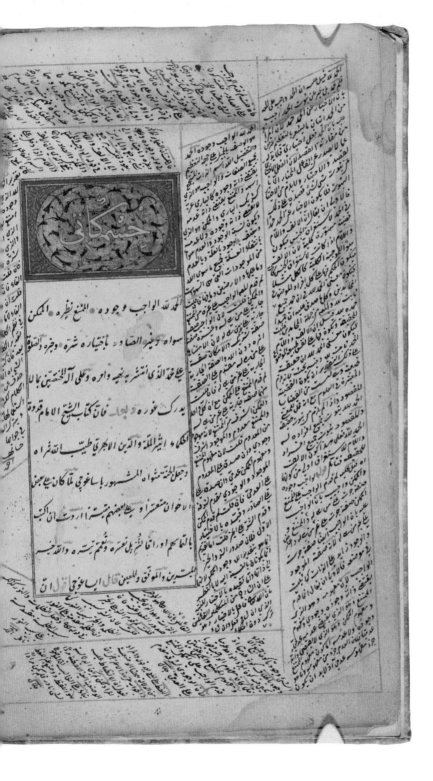

Terry Tempest Williams

with Emma Lewis

Aaron Siskind's
Utah Series

On Grief, Ravens, and the Desert's Vibrations

TERRY TEMPEST WILLIAMS   I think there's a beautiful correspondence between the Harvard Divinity School and the Graduate School of Design.

EMMA LEWIS   Yes, especially for people thinking about sacred space and what that can mean and look like.

TTW   And also the question of what it means to design a conscious life, internally and externally. How are we designing for both our needs and desires in ways that contribute to the angst and the well-being of this moment? I think, on some level, these questions all have to do with constructing space.

EL   You ask a beautiful question in your book *Erosion*, in the interview with your friend Tim DeChristopher, "What do you love?" I'm wondering how you would answer that.

TTW   I've been thinking about touch. So much of this pandemic has been about being touched: being touched by the suffering of others, being touched by grief and wondering how to express our grief, individually and collectively, for the losses surrounding us. Grief is love. I wonder about what will happen if we don't "touch" our grief and if we continue to ignore it, push it away.
    Before our call, I was out walking, and the ravens were just going wild, soaring and cavorting with the breeze as a storm moved in. Allowing ourselves to be touched—by the wind, by sunlight, or by birdsong—is a gift. Being touched by the seasons, being touched by daily phone conversations with my father, who's 88 years old, sitting down for a meal with my husband Brooke. This is how I am thinking about love: keeping in touch.
    The pandemic has sent us home and brought us to our knees. I appreciate the personal recognition, being forced to realize I don't want to be moving so fast in the world anymore.

195

I want to be home. I want to have time for a cup of tea or a conversation like the one we are having now. That's what I'm loving and learning in the midst of the terror and uncertainty. How do we hold one another in this moment of a global pandemic? Is it not enough to ask each other, "What do you love?" like you asked me, or "How are you, *truly*?" or "What might we create together that will be beautiful?"

EL   And asking, "Are we brave enough to fail together as we try?"

TTW   Exactly. What is the work that is ours? On one hand, it's staying alive. On another, it's being present with our vote or showing up with whatever gift is ours. For the first time in my life, Emma, I feel like a writer. I feel that my pen during this pandemic has been my shovel, and I show up every single day and work. I have said yes to everything. Normally, I am more selective, but the smallest *yes* can loom large in ways we can't anticipate.

EL   I want to ask about your work as a writer, conservationist, and activist defending Bears Ears National Monument in southeastern Utah. What has that work been like for you, and what do you think is needed now from people who are designers, especially urban planners, landscape architects, and architects?

TTW   Bears Ears and the establishment of Bears Ears National Monument has been such a crucial education for me as a white conservationist in the state of Utah. To learn to step to the side and be an ally; to follow the leadership of Indigenous people in the American Southwest, particularly the five tribes of this region, the Diné (Navajo), Hopi, Zuni, Ute Mountain Ute, and Ouray Ute; to follow their leads, to listen, to offer support if needed; to acknowledge different ways of "designing" political and personal strategies while "building" inclusive models of power and sustaining relationships. It has been very moving. Listening to the elders when they say, "These are not just public lands, these are our ancestral lands," opens up a deeper conversation. Sacred land protection takes on a different tone honoring the complexities of tribal histories.

I have also been moved by the generosity of spiritual leaders like Jonah Yellowman who has said, "We are not just protecting Bears Ears for our people, but all people." There is an emphasis on healing rather than on the drama surrounding political power. Obama listened to the voices of tribal leaders

TERRY TEMPEST WILLIAMS WITH EMMA LEWIS

Utah 90 1975

aaron Siskind

and Native elders in this region and honored them by establishing Bears Ears National Monument in 2016 through the 1906 Antiquities Act. Less than a year later, Donald Trump gutted the Bears Ears National Monument by 85 percent. He saw these sacred lands only as real estate that could garner huge amounts of money and opened it up for oil and gas development. It was a brutal act of disrespect and dismissal of Native Peoples.

I remember saying to Willie Grayeyes, now a county commissioner from Navajo Mountain, "What do you do with your anger?" He looked at me and said, "It can no longer be about anger, it has to be about healing." I asked him what he meant. "We have to go to the source of our pain," he said, "so our wounds can heal." All of ours. I think that's really a fundamental question to ask when you're designing anything. What is the source of our pain in places that have been broken by treaties, by promises, by racism, or by invisibility and cruelty?

EL   I'm drawn to the idea that identifying pain and its sources can lead not only to a deeper sense of that pain but also to a reimagination and clearer understanding of what's most needed now.

TTW   These communities in the Navajo Nation Indian country like Monument Valley and Westwater, outside Blanding, Utah—they don't have water, Emma. At Goulding's Lodge, where tens of thousands of tourists come to stay every year, they have all the water imaginable, showers for everyone. Where Jonah lives or where Willie lives, there is no running water or plumbing. Hopefully, this will change soon. The Utah legislature has finally responded, but the changes are not coming soon enough. The pandemic was proof of the need for these kinds of human rights in the United States of America.

So that's one thing they're thinking about, what kinds of water systems are sustainable in the desert, especially in a megadrought. They're looking at cisterns, and they're also looking at windmills. And how to develop a windmill with solar energy that can pump water up from an already declining aquifer. Given the severity of drought and fires in the midst of climate change, the American Southwest is going to be one of the hardest hit areas anywhere in the world. Last summer, we had two inches of water precipitation. The average is ten inches. I put two inches in a cup. That is a sip in a very big country.

There are so many design opportunities with regard to climate instability, especially in rural America. But in the

Utah 245 1975

Aaron Siskind

199

American Southwest, the urgency now is water and constructing a life that conserves water and meets the needs of the people, all people, especially in Native communities.

EL   I wonder if there could be some space for grieving—for the denial of necessary resources in Native communities, for irreparable ecological losses tied to climate change—and if that space could actually provide the energy that's needed for transformation and justice.

TTW   You know what I would love to see the GSD do in this time of COVID? I see it in Indian country and in our own communities. I think we need to design monuments for grieving. We are now approaching 300,000 citizens who have died, and there's hardly a mention. Yesterday, we reached the highest death rate we've had: over 3,000. As a design student, as a school of design, what would monuments for grieving look like during the pandemic?

EL   Yes, and how can we move through the landscapes of our lives carrying our grief? Or, how can we walk through our grief as a shared experience that can lead to healing? I wish for that too.

TTW   I love that. You know, I lost my brother to suicide two years ago, and someone asked, "When do you ever get over your grief?" I said, "It's been my experience that you walk with grief every day. It's the raven on my shoulder." But when you asked how we walk through our grief—I think that's something different. I want to think about that, Emma, that is so powerful. What would that look and feel like? How would we experience that together? Grief is so private, and yet I feel like what we're missing is the experience of walking through our grief in public.

EL   What I love in your work is how you're able to bear witness to what's beautiful and also to what's most difficult and painful. I wonder if you have any words about building up that practice of listening and the ability to maintain presence with what challenges us.

TTW   There is a stillness in the desert that demands it be listened to. It's beyond silence. It is vibrational. There's something about the silence of deep time that is held in the rocks, and the silence heard in the aftermath of wind. The silence of drought is terrifying because it portends death.

There is the silence that is disrupted by the wing beats of ravens. I'm always aware of the stillness, the silences in this landscape. To me, it is erosional, capable of cracking stone. It's part of the erosional landscape that takes us to the essence of things.

The Red Rock Desert calms my soul; it restores a silence and stillness in me. Whenever I come home after being in Cambridge, I'm met by this silence. You slow down and pay attention to the world in a different way. You listen. Last night we heard there would be Northern Lights visible across the country. We went outside to see if we could hear the Northern Lights because we had once heard them in the Arctic. They sounded like Tibetan bells and singing bowls.

The desert is all about listening: listening to the coyotes, listening to the voices of piñon jays as they gather in flocks of hundreds, listening to meadowlarks call to one another in the spring. We heard the songs of the bluebirds yesterday. I haven't known them to stay through the winter. Listening to the roar of the Colorado River or the eddies or the flat water, knowing the different chords of the way water moves—it's all part of residency in the desert. Being in nature, being in wild places, listening is a matter of survival. I think listening to each other, especially now, is also about survival. Where is our common ground if not beneath our feet?

EL   Yes. I like the idea of listening for the silences that exist within a physical landscape and that being a pathway to recognizing spaces of silence within ourselves and within other people.

TTW   That's such a good point, Emma. When I think about love, it's full of silences, silences that can be generative and soul-saving. There can also be a generosity about silence that speaks of respect.

Silences can also be a cruelty or even a violence. Silence too often follows abuse, and people get hurt when we don't speak out. There are the deafening silences, the silences when one realizes who is not seated around this table and whose voice is being silenced intentionally. Our relationship to silence and listening is how we learn to speak; perhaps, this is the path to finding our own voices.

EL   I'm thinking of the writing you've done about the way rock formations seem silent to us when in fact there's so much sound and vibration emerging from them. I wonder about

201

Utah 21 1976   Aaron Siskind

TERRY TEMPEST WILLIAMS WITH EMMA LEWIS

Utah 180 1975   Aaron Siskind

seeking out that which seems silent and then questioning it or finding new ways of listening through it.

TTW That's so beautiful. What's your sense of listening in silence?

EL My sense is that it's the work of life. My sense is that it's beautiful to try, that it can be difficult. I think there can be a sense of perilousness in true listening. It demands a willingness to be transformed by what you hear, by what you hadn't known or felt before.

TTW Yes. You make me think about the silences of grief, and, in contrast, what a keening is. I remember in Rwanda, on the day of mourning in April on the anniversary of the genocide, the keening. The wailing you heard from the women whose children had been murdered was almost too much to bear. The women were only allowed to express their grief publicly on that day of that month. The rest of the year they lived in the silences of their own grief.

EL So much is present with us all the time, including different voices. We encounter something—maybe a song, a place, another person—and it can open spaces in us that we didn't know were speaking.
Can we talk about the photographs I sent you?

TTW When you sent me the photographs, they startled me, and that got my attention. They were so foreign to what I know living here; they looked like isolated body parts to me, and they reached me like oil, which doesn't make sense, I know. It was a tactile response without thought. I realized just how saturated my visual landscape is by color and light, and so to be thrust back all of a sudden into a world of black and white stationary patterns and visual and intellectual subtleties threw me.
I went into Siskind's archives and found a photograph of Castleton Tower, which is where we live. I look at this geologic feature every day. In a sense, the photographs you sent brought me back home in a way I'd never seen before, a way outside of color, outside of the familiar. Now as we are talking, I see this is like the pandemic.
Siskind's images remind me of what endures. That photograph of Castleton must have been taken decades ago, and yet it's what we see every night: the freestanding silhouette when the light has gone into the domain of the moon. Siskind's photographs also seem so beautifully tied to design. They're

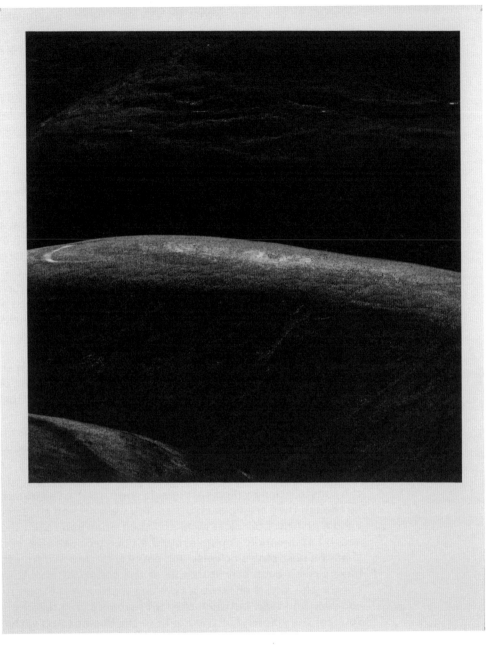

AARON SISKIND'S *UTAH* SERIES

reimagined landscapes that defy scale. They're playful and dissonant: forms become a disruption or a disturbance of representation. They invite creativity. Nothing is as it appears. How do you see them?

EL   I imagine Siskind moving through the landscape and making choices about how to attend to it. A designer makes similar choices about what to attend to now and what to create from that. These questions lead to futures where we can return and notice differently. So, I see an invitation.

TTW   I love that. I love that you asked us to contemplate these images together. To keep stretching our capacity to see, to imagine is so crucial to being alive. Thank you. You know, a friend of mine, Barry Lopez, passed away recently. I met him when I was 24. He was a mentor of mine, and ours was a long and transformative friendship. He died on Christmas Day, and I think of him often. He spoke about the power of gesture, and how even in drought, "someone has to dance the dance of the long-legged bird to bring back the river." I am paraphrasing, but it is the notion that what we do matters. Ceremony matters. Ritual matters.

Some friends of ours in Castle Valley, including Sarah Hedden, a woman who's an architect and a practitioner of tea, came together on the winter solstice in a Daoist ritual called a "star walk."

You take the constellation of the Big Dipper—you look up, and there it is in the night sky—and recreate it on the ground by setting candles on the snow, each light representing a star in the constellation. You then create another configuration of the constellation by flipping it upside down next to the others as though they cradle each other. You walk around the first candle or first star clockwise, and then when you reach the second star-candle you go around it counterclockwise, and then the next star clockwise and counterclockwise until you have circled each starlit candle of the constellations that mirror the sky. It creates a spinning motion within you as you walk and twirl between the two reversed constellations. You feel the spinning of the Earth in the cosmos and within your body, and yet there is a stillness of space and time being nurtured inside and outside of you.

Each one of us engaged with the star walk alone. It became a walking meditation, and then we returned to the bonfire in the desert. It was one of those beautiful moments, a solitude shared, where you feel rearranged by the honoring of what's

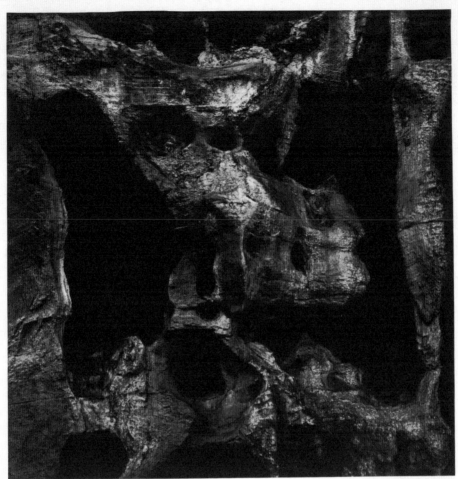

Utah 53 1976   Aaron Siskind

happening cosmologically. It really was a design that choreographed an internal shift by setting up parameters for us to move through externally.

EL   That seems like such an act of love to me, being able to identify a constellation with this kind of care and to follow that form even when there are other constellations and countless stars.

TTW   And did I mention it was part of the Saturn–Jupiter conjunction? It really was magical and, you're right, an act of love. Now that I've gone back to Siskind's photographs, I find them such a comfort, to see beyond the obvious, to go from the real to the abstract, to the more sensual, to the more gritty. It brought me back to the essence of things. It makes me return to the idea that we were discussing, of what a memorial for grieving might look like figuratively. What's the vibration, what are the patterns, what is the abstraction that could be made real in one's heart? I just keep returning to that idea, and here we are now almost at 400,000 deaths of fellow citizens.

EL   I'm looking at one of the photographs on my screen and thinking about how to be really immersed in something that can be dark and difficult, how to really see it and not look away.

TTW   I want to read you this, from the essay "Love in a Time of Terror," one of the last things Barry Lopez wrote: "... in this moment, is it still possible to face the gathering darkness, and say to the physical Earth, and to all its creatures, including ourselves, fiercely and without embarrassment, I love you, and to embrace fearlessly the burning world?"

EL   It's beautiful. I'm recalling this earlier question: "What do you love?" I hope that by asking this of ourselves and of others we can begin to say, "I want to embrace this, and I can love this," or that we can recognize the ways that we're already loving and in love. When we experience losses, how can we remain both deeply in a state of loss and deeply in a state of love?

TTW   I'm looking out the window, and Castleton Tower is bright orange! There's a rock formation called the Priest and Nuns and then Castleton Tower, a 400-foot sandstone monolith. There are diagonal lines of snow on the red sand base, little squiggly lines of snow that haven't melted yet. It's so beautiful. I love this hour of encore light, the last light of day. The shadows moving across the valley in this sea of sage and juniper, shadows walking up that slope to the top of Castleton Tower, and then it will be twilight. First stars appear. But there's something about the primary colors—this burnt orange against a turquoise sky—that is just so luminous right now.

EL   You mentioned earlier that there was a rockslide near you recently, that it woke you up in the middle of the night. I'm thinking of both together: the abundance of color and shapes and shifting shadows that you just described and then also the total darkness and unexpected crumbling that strikes fear.

TTW   Yes. We heard the sound like a bomb in the night, but we fell back to sleep, thinking we had been dreaming. In the morning, we awoke to fresh snow. The rockslide appeared blood red on the white slope. You would see the shear on the cliff, how part of the rock face fell in a movement more akin to water than rock. If the snow hadn't been there, we would have missed the pattern of the trajectory; it would have all just blended into the sandstone rubble, and we might not have noticed it at all. The snow showed us the formation of falling, and the force and velocity of that kind of breaking.

Of course, things are always being hidden, but so much is coming to the fore, and in a way, that's the gift. This is an extraordinary moment of reckoning and awakening, erosion and evolution. You can't have one without the other. In the midst of the terror and the weight of this pandemic, all of it, seen and unseen, I keep returning to gratitude and a prayer that I can stay present and continue to stare it down—"it" being the uncertainty, my fears, and isolation. Even if something is disturbing or unsettling, like Siskind's photos were at first to me, to know that something can come back to you in ways that will sustain you, this may be a moment of return. What we return to is up to each of us.

Emma, I'm looking again at the first image that you sent me. When I first saw it I thought, "My god, it's a monster," and then I thought, "No, it's a pelvic bone." Today I see it as a temple. I see two entry points, almost like portals.

Jane Mah Hutton

with Maxwell Smith-Holmes

New England Erratics

On Cultural Geology and Erratic Personalities

MAXWELL SMITH-HOLMES   What are we looking at?

JANE MAH HUTTON   This photograph from the Gardner Collection of Photos, formerly of the Harvard geology department, is titled "Tilting Rock, Massachusetts" and shows a man posing next to an erratic boulder that is definitely tilting. It was part of an exhibition at the GSD in 2010 called *Erratics: A Genealogy of Rock Landscape*, which also featured the work of Claude Cormier Architectes Paysagistes. It came together with Charles Waldheim's original framing, Dan Borelli's amazing exhibition team, and Mary Daniels's (of Loeb Library) immense knowledge of nearby archives and cultural geology, along with many others. The exhibition was about how landscape architects have worked with rocks not as stone surfaces or stone walls but as references to geological elements and formations. Rocks for rocks sake.

    The exhibition connected projects of this kind by landscape architects from the last few decades—from Peter Walker and SWA Group's Tanner Fountain of erratic boulders at the Harvard Science Center to Ken Smith's plastic rocks in the MoMA Roof Garden—to lineages of cultural geology. This included looking at the role that erratic boulders played in art, popular culture, and the theorization of global glaciation in the 19th century. Because erratic boulders are different geological matter than the bedrock they sit on, they served as evidence that they came from somewhere else.

MSH   Do you know anything about the human figure in the photo?

JMH   I don't, but when looking at many portraits of erratic boulders, I became interested in how people had documented them and especially how they posed near or on them. Even in the most sober scientific recordings of them, people were hamming it up nearby. They were scale figures but also lounging, climbing,

Man leaning against "Tilting Rock" in Annisquam, Gloucester, Massachusetts, 189x. Gardner Collection of Photographs No. 4089.

JANE MAH HUTTON WITH MAXWELL SMITH-HOLMES

or just striking a pose, like this guy. The photos of boulders are not only scientific documentation but also cultural artifacts: they become characters in themselves.

MSH   What kinds of personalities do the rocks have?

JMH   Good question! I think that what interested me in the photographs of the erratics is that while it was the mass distribution of erratics all over the globe that made them evidence of global change, the photos focus on individual rocks as characters. I think it has something to do with their size, which is often huge to a person but perhaps more physically approachable than other geological phenomena. People named them, including settlers as they took land across the continent, and, as the author Jamaica Kincaid writes about garden plants, "to name is to possess." We can see how this naming of rocks, towns, and land was a form of colonial possession and dispossession, overwriting Indigenous names, access to land, and relationships to it. With help from Senta Burton, I gathered, mapped, and wrote about culturally identified erratics that were deposited after the last glacial period for Elizabeth Ellsworth and Jamie Kruse's edited book, *Making the Geologic Now*, and for Etienne Turpin's edited book, *Architecture in the Anthropocene*.

MSH   How do elements such as rocks act as evidence? Do they leave clues as to how the landscape might be the scene of a crime?

JMH   They were evidence in plain sight. You look out on your farm and you see rocks strewn everywhere. The shared knowledge about them around the world is what enabled these theories to develop through slowly gathering daily observations. But their cultural adoption also is evidence: of land grabbing, of land marking, or of a specific community's desire to memorialize a place or event. For me, this is a helpful metaphor for almost any research. It means I can pick up anything and start to use that as a door into larger stories about where things come from and what that means at different scales.

Looking at material samples, for instance, has led me to really want to know how they connect to other places, so I started to think about everything as evidence. There's nothing you can look at that doesn't become evidence for its own making. It almost sounds too simple—*of course, that's the case*—but that's not how I was used to seeing things before. I was used to seeing them as they were sold to me or as I specified them—as commodities and products.

213

Beach, Gay Head, Massachusetts, looking south, 189x. Jotham A. French. Gardner Collection of Photographs No. 4611.

JANE MAH HUTTON WITH MAXWELL SMITH-HOLMES

It's a connection between something that's very personal, like, let's say, at the scale of our immediate experience. Like something we're touching, something we have some kind of relationship to. Something that is easy to think we're not connected to. There's actually evidence of a specific type of mining right here on my desk, in my pen and my hard drive.

MSH   It is interesting to compare these named erratics, which occur naturally but take on cultural dimensions, with anthropogenic landforms, like the island of plastic in the Pacific Ocean, which are produced by human culture but take on geological properties.

JMH   These boulders are not anthropogenic, but they're made cultural, right? The Plymouth Rock is not not-human. It's got a lot of cultural baggage. Maybe for the same reason, the kind of landforms like plastic islands are helpful things to identify and discuss, to draw our attention toward. There's plastic everywhere. There's plastic pollution in every everywhere. But in that island we can see it, it's named, it's a single thing and useful as a symbolic element. Of course, it's a physical crisis that needs addressing in a pragmatic way, but it's also a way to get people's minds wrapped around something that's very difficult to understand.

I think what's interesting about all of these things—something landscape architects are concerned with too—is how to represent something changing when you're called on to represent space in a single state.

How can you possibly convey all of this deepness—deep movement, deep time—in a single frame? Erratics are there, they're really heavy, so you cannot move them easily, but we know that they've traveled. We know that in this particular moment we see them in a place, but we also know they came from somewhere else. They are like a vehicle for making that connection, which is otherwise very difficult to make. We know everything around us is in a flow even though it doesn't look like it.

MSH   If it is so difficult to capture these kinds of flows in static images, do you think a closer relationship to materiality would help us understand the complexities of the world? With everything taking place online nowadays, it seems we are getting even further from the dynamic processes of cities, landscapes, and buildings. I am asking this question in part because I heard that you had a role in the Loeb Library Materials Collection.

215

JMH   Yes, I had a great time working with Alix Reiskind and Johanna Kasubowski, and we talked a lot about how to bring the Visual and Materials Collections together to activate them and see them with new eyes. We often think of the materials as "new" and the visuals as "historic documents," but there is so much richness when you break those categories down. We'd try things like bringing photographs from the collection of forestry together with wood samples to conjure their connection, that kind of thing.

I think it is true that drawing is often a mediation that is one step of distance from materiality, but drawing has its own materiality and power. I think it's very helpful to have some contact with materials. I find it really interesting when people are drawing with earth or trying to somehow mix these different kinds of traditional and found media. In the studios that I'm working with right now, we're often trying to make models that involve nonrepresentational materials; it's imperfect and it doesn't work to scale and is messy and all kinds of other things. Right now, I find that stimulating and fun and a nice counterpart to the orthographic representation I've been accustomed to.

Emanuel Admassu

with Kyle Winston

"After Property" Studio Imagery

On the Edge of the Discipline

EMANUEL ADMASSU   So, just to clarify the studio's structure—

KYLE WINSTON   Sure.

EA   The students started working individually and identified what we called "samples." Basically, the samples are ideas of spatial practice that work outside the logics of property. The students had to present them, iterate, and argue for them. Then, a few weeks in, we switched. So, you might be the person who sampled it, but someone else inherits it and iterates on it. The whole ambition was that the samples would produce a collective catalog that could be shared across the studio.

The "After Property" studio held in the fall of 2020 included students Bailey Brown, Michele Chen, Kyat Chin, Olivia Howard, Kathlyn Kao, Keira Li, Caleb Negash, Isaac Pollan, Diandra Rendradjaja, Sam Sheffer, Yifei Wu, and Cindy Yiin.

Separate to this, the students also analyzed a specific site that they considered to be emblematic of the regime of property. At some point, the sites became hybridized because the students worked in pairs after first working individually from both the samples and the sites.

Kyle   I was considering giving you bits of my talk with Emanuel, but I thought instead to keep these conversations—

KW   When the images changed hands, were they supposed to be read naively? Or did the students also hand over some baggage, including loaded meanings or political intent behind the images?

Caleb   Untainted.

Kyle   Exactly.

EA   They did, yeah. And the second person obviously modified the image in response to their own interests. I think the way Kyat iterated an image, for example, leaned closer to a typical architectural representation conversation and less into the maroon communities that were represented in the book cover Caleb started with. So, we were also really interested in what gets lost in translation as ideas get handed over.

Kyat   A lot of our speculations started from drawings —Emanuel categorized them as "samples" and "sites"— where we explored the dismantling of property, which is typically very rigid.

KW   To talk through a couple of other images: in her brief presentation, Kathy discussed questions of permanence and its connection to property.

219

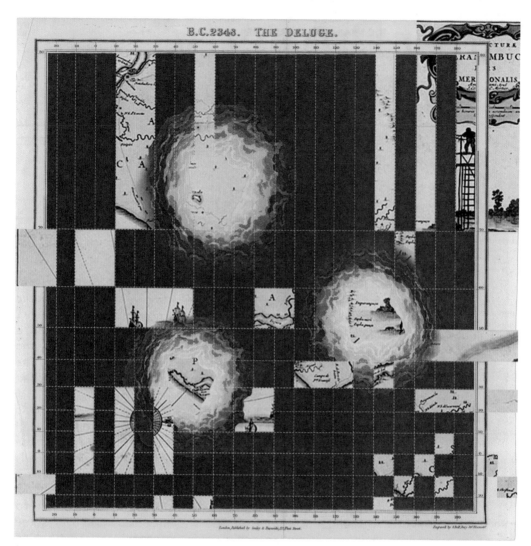

Olivia   We had to locate or create images that represented the issues dealt with in the texts we were assigned. This was a way of transferring conceptual ideas and starting to spatialize them into visual registers.

"Cartographic Clouds," a collaborative project "sample." The project asks, "How can representational and topological strategies of indeterminacy obscure and disrupt the regime of property?" Finished by Olivia Howard and Caleb Negash, fall 2020.

EMANUEL ADMASSU WITH KYLE WINSTON

She was really interested in ephemeral structures, like tents, and how people can deploy them to claim space. Whenever there is a form of state surveillance or surveillance from the "propertied" class, if you will, one is able to shift the position of their ephemeral structure. So, we were talking a lot about space-claiming strategies, especially by Indigenous communities, and how each strategy comes out of a certain form of protest. At other times, it's actually the way people prefer to live. There are communities that are not necessarily seeking permanence.

KW

Bailey presented on what she called "Uneven Ground," recontextualizing police auction objects in a gallery setting on an earthen floor.

EA

Olivia For example, we looked at a type of traditional Indonesian architecture that centers around a hearth, but we were trying not to just take that image of the lifestyle and have it be representative of or translatable into something else. We were instead trying to identify frameworks, strategies, and operatives in order to ask, what are the things that have a concrete identifiable history, and then, what are the things that we can apply to our own projects based on that context?

Bailey's analysis centered on the work of Cameron Rowland, who is probably the most interesting artist thinking about property right now. Each of these images are kind of snapshots from his art practice merged with Walter De Maria's *The Earth Room*, which at some point entered into the conversation.

One of Rowland's most brilliant art pieces doesn't deal directly with carceral labor but with how the prison industrial complex is used to reproduce notions of property. He identified a particular site in North Carolina (which used to be a plantation) and purchased it with a nonprofit that he established. He then made this radical proposal of saying that the only act of reparation is not just giving this land back to Black people, but actually removing it from the regime of property. He established a land trust that maintains the value of that land at $0. Forever. So basically, there's nothing you can do to make that land property anymore.

KW

In another sample, Kira's image of a Harlem street feels like a Dalí landscape. The city stoop looks hot and seems to melt and swirl like ice cream.

EA

Yeah, we were having these discussions about the limits of the everyday and how there's a moment when it becomes somewhat surreal. This slippage between what is considered to be ordinary and what is somewhat mythical.

A lot of the discussion was really about street culture and what it means to extend the domestic realm. Usually, that is a decision made because the domestic realm has been squeezed by the logic of speculative real estate. In this case, the street became a living room through Kira's reinterpretation.

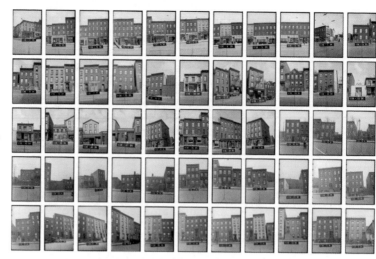

Bailey The word "sample" was used instead of "precedent," which was helpful because we were able to pull from a ton of different sources. For example, Sam was looking at Hurricane Katrina refugee victim cots as a way out of property but also as a definition of it. Later on, I pulled a sample of little shade tents that are erected on college campuses, claiming space with individual property while breaking down institutional property. We found samples that are not inherently architectural. This is what Emanuel pulled out of us: not precedents to property but a way out.

Keira To go one step further, we took an image and manipulated it to speculate on how, for example, people construct the notion of a home in the context of renderings of luxury apartments.

"The Redacted Block" project on the Brooklyn brownstone and property tax record photography, which shows that in 1940, the documentation of a Prospect Heights block was comprehensive, but by 1980 the set was highly deficient. This suggests those unrecorded properties in this majority African-American neighborhood were blighted and in need of governmental intervention. Image compilation by Kathlyn Kao and Cindy Yiin, fall 2020.

KW   Assuming she isn't from Harlem and that most of the students were just introduced to these subjects and sites, were the texts supposed to be a way in?

EA   Yeah, definitely. The Saidiya Hartman and Tina Campt readings on the site were particularly influential here because I don't know if Kira's been to Harlem. That's part of the challenge.

KW   I thought about that a lot in the studio presentations: how do you construct your own site? I guess that's always a challenge in school to some extent. If we haven't been there, we have to act like we know.

EA   Yeah, and I don't think that's unique to the COVID condition. That's the condition of our discipline. Anyone who is practicing internationally is forced to operate under those constraints. A lot of it is based on learning how to read images and learning how to be in conversation with people who are not in the room. So, I think the attempt here was to learn about Harlem from people who have really engaged with the neighborhood in a profound way.

Yifei Zillow, for example, represents housing in a very similar way for every type of space, such as in the renderings of units in tall residential towers. We were trying to tackle representation with representation.

KW   In Caleb and Olivia's presentation, the reviewers were enamored by the unwillingness of the drawings to follow any

EMANUEL ADMASSU WITH KYLE WINSTON

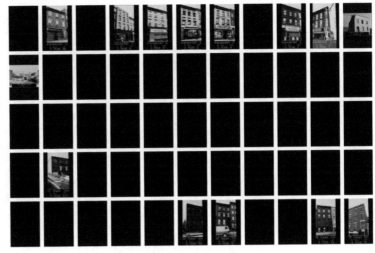

Kyle So, the process is about a belief in representation as a catalyst for thinking about real ramifications? You're thinking, if we draw it differently, the opposite will be true?

Michele I think it's reciprocal. We need to first change the way we understand what we're looking at and then draw it differently. That's what is going to stimulate other understandings. I think this is why Emanuel wanted us to produce the images.

conventional rules of architectural representation. Can you talk about this a bit?

EA

Sam With an image, I do think there is a certain generative quality. Bailey spoke to the intoxication of this quality, and I totally agree with that too, but there's also this quality that can be interpreted in many ways by many people who are not necessarily architects, which is very important.

This came out of a long struggle. In the end, it became really clear that the only way you can represent the phenomenon they're interested in—the cartographic representation of the Quilombo of Palmares, a settlement of escaped slaves in Brazil, and their present-day relationship to the "heritage–industrial complex"—is by refusing legibility. It was an exercise of erasing the mapping of the site rather than actually drawing it. They presented the hesitation that they had being positioned here in New England while representing a site in Brazil, which is highly contested and has its own complex history. At some point, they ran into the limits of their positionality in relation to the site.

KW

Diandra One of the struggles in representation was to choose "the money shot." In typical architectural representation, you usually have one cool rendering, but here, that one image isn't enough. A constellation of images is what actually matters. And that's funny because what we were proposing was a constellation of networks. That was the "project" and it carried through to the representation. Without those images, it wouldn't add up to the same argument.

There were terms that came up over and over during the reviews, which all seem to be related, such as the term illegibility in this project, as well as refusal, opacity, redaction, misuse, redefinition, ruination. They're all very "in the negative" or reactionary to an extent.

Looking at these terms alongside the manifesto written by you and the Black Reconstruction Collective, there's a line that explains how a nation in conflict with its own ideals would need to "be reconstructed before it can fully be constructed." So, I see a theme here. These terms are capturing a kind of destabilization of the status quo. But I'm wondering, can we just be reactionary? What's after illegibility?

Caleb Olivia and I had a lot of anxiety about fetishizing or idealizing this Maroon community of people who had escaped slavery. This was also related to the idea that drawing always flattens and tries to contain or describe. We learned there are other ways of mapping and representing that are based entirely on different worldviews.

Kathlyn There is this lurking tension between what it means to be a designer and to be talking about marginalized peoples. I think the fact that in our project we say "design for" is problematic, and we never came to a conclusion on how to give agency to others. How do you deal with the power that we as architects hold?

"The Redacted Block" project image exploring neighborhood bodies and the "spatialization of control." Created by Kathlyn Kao and Cindy Yiin, fall 2020.

EA

Isaac In my life, architecture has always (or almost always) been a protagonist and I don't think that the studio was necessarily saying that all architecture is bad, but it assumed it a little, implying that architecture is dangerous until proven otherwise.

Caleb Somebody in the review expressed that maybe the way to frame this is not necessarily extractive. It's not about what we are trying to learn from or take from this historical practice we're studying, it's more about figuring out a way to study that material closely and find a way to make it more legible in spatial or architectural terms.

There's so much work that needs to be done in the realm of reconstruction, in the realm of disassembly. A lot of the energy right now is invested in understanding how oppressive the structures that we operate within are and attempting to take them apart. I don't want to understate that work because I think it is, in some ways, an endless project. The larger structures we're discussing, if you're talking about racial capitalism, will always recalibrate themselves and come back as something else. Every time you think you've disassembled them and you've won, they've actually mutated into something more powerful. You can trace this throughout the history of this country from slavery to Jim Crow to redlining to the prison industrial complex. They are always mutating and becoming something more powerful and more sinister in a way, something that is much harder to detect.

The most interesting people thinking about these issues now are operating from this realm of refusal. We borrowed that term loosely from the Practicing Refusal Collective, which was started by Tina Campt and Saidiya Hartman. Mabel Wilson,

EMANUEL ADMASSU WITH KYLE WINSTON

one of the curators of the recent MoMA show *Reconstructions: Architecture and Blackness in America*, is also a member. They speak about this practice of refusal because these structures are always going to have a prominent presence in your life. You have to always position yourself in opposition to them. I think that sensibility really comes from the frustration of having to deal with that for generations, for centuries. Simultaneously, I think these practices of refusal are always imaginative. They're always imagining a completely different type of world. I think what is interesting about this position of negating the status quo is that you're automatically producing something else.

So, the moment you reject gravity, you need to find a way to float, right?

I think that's the part that gets lost in these conversations sometimes because people think you're just reacting against and you're not reacting for. But actually you're reacting for human dignity and you're reacting for a more equitable society. If anything, it's much more optimistic than the tendency we have as architects to run back into the realm of autonomy and say, "Hey, we're just over here doing these really sexy floor plans." Instead of that, this is saying, "I'm going to engage with the world very directly. And, I'm going to engage with it with a certain level of criticality that is aware of its history, that is aware of the current conditions, etc."

KW   Do you think the binary is important? The status quo and then its refusal?

EA   We're really interested in reconstruction because it's saying, "Hey, we have to make a new world." That making of a new world will obviously require the replacement of the world that has been causing so much violence and dispossession.

But, I would be careful. I don't know if your formulation is accurate enough because I think these are two practices that always have to occur simultaneously. You basically can't do one without the other. You have to deal with history, and you also have to imagine a future, and if you try to do one without the other, then you fall into the same traps of previous generations of artists and architects.

KW   What was your motivation for teaching this studio?

EA   Witnessing everything that we've been collectively witnessing; through our phones, through our laptops. The constant negation of Black life is fundamental to the reason why I decided to do this studio. I didn't want to do one of those studios that was

"AFTER PROPERTY" STUDIO IMAGERY

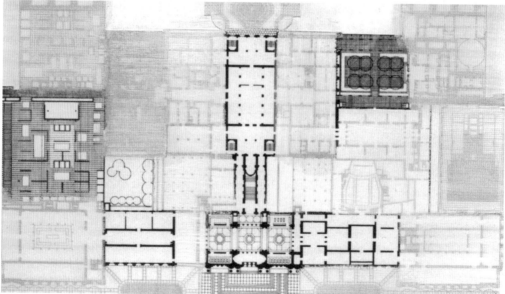

He also very gra-
ciously called us out. Emanuel
explained to us, "You're going
to end up with something
mediocre if you don't work
independently first and
then come together from the
experimental work."

"After Met" project imagery probing the "inherent contradictions between the
societal value of a museum and the oppressive and exclusive regime of property."
The Metropolitan Museum of Art is a "celebration of a diversity of cultures"
albeit one built on the "tireless seizure of resources and cultural heritage." Created
by Isaac Pollan and Diandra Rendradjaja, fall 2020.

like, "Oh, let's come up with anti-racist strategies." Instead this studio asked, "What is fundamental to this value system?" Because we're looking at 500 years of history, and property is fundamental to the discipline of architecture. I'm definitely not alone in thinking about this. We need to really talk about property and how the definition keeps changing.

KW   In the studio's syllabus you describe pulling from the visual arts as a way to push what we think of as our typical representational means in architecture. Do you think the visual arts are more disentangled from property?

EA   I think a lot of contemporary artists, especially conceptual artists, are finding ways to challenge these regimes in much more complex and nuanced ways than we have been able to do as architects because, as architects, we fundamentally make property. And in my opinion, at least for the past 10 years (if not the past 60 or 80), the discipline of architecture has taken a defensive posture. At best, there's been a certain level of criticality that is directed toward saying, "Hey, this is the world order, and we're just surfing it."

Keira   I liked the studio because it was speculative. It encouraged us to think less about the material constraints in real life, because in reality we can't really get rid of property. It's important to think about all of architecture's potential.

KW   Such as pointing to developers and saying the power is actually with them.

EA   Yeah. I mean, there is some truth to that. I have an architecture practice with my partner Jen Wood where we mostly make buildings, and I do believe in the potential of buildings to basically provide space for radically different regimes. For example, a building that was designed for a socialist regime can easily be co-opted by a capitalist one and vice versa. So, there is an openness to making buildings. But architecture as a discipline and as a discourse has been too shy to really push the limits of that openness.

KW   Do you distinguish making buildings from the discipline of architecture?

EA   The discipline is way more than making buildings. That's why we're engaged in producing knowledge that is tied to spatial practices. To me, that's the definition of architecture I'm most comfortable with. Because architecture is a form of knowledge more than a profession. It requires us to make models, to make drawings, to write essays, but it's really about engaging with some sort of public discourse around spatial practices. Making buildings is a subset of that and an important subset

227

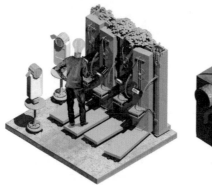

Caleb And to think about how disciplinary silos are only useful until they're not. Our focus is not about asking whether or not architects are the best people to tackle questions of representation and property, but rather about acknowledging that we can't really do it alone. I would say that someone in another discipline isn't better equipped, but that projects are better done among or between different disciplines.

Cindy Architecture doesn't exist in a vacuum. That was really what I think the studio was trying to push through—resist compartmentalizing.

"Re-Imagining the Capitalist Game" project imagery exploring the Pruitt-Igoe development, which reinterprets the "architectural elements of unitization, symbolizing the capitalist control over property"—like those of the Monopoly game board—as sampled from a now wild, ruinous, and newly liberated site. Created by Michele Chen and Keira Li, fall 2020.

of it. But I wouldn't say it's the core of architecture. The ideas that surround the buildings are much more powerful than the buildings themselves.

KW I'm not necessarily disagreeing, but for whom? For culture at large, for students, or for practitioners? I see the ideas that you're instilling in your students, and then I see the drawings, the images, and I'm wondering, "Who is this for?" I think you also care about architecture because of its different audiences, right? There's a disciplinary audience, and there's the larger public. You just mentioned public discourses, which suggests architecture's civic role. If we're talking about knowledge creation, who is this knowledge for?

Olivia It's a matter of what the discipline needs to bring in order to change but also what the discipline needs to export in order to free itself. If we can export mapping to other disciplines, then maybe the legacy of what colonial cartography has resulted in will change.

EA I mean, that's it! What you just said. It's trying to be a civic project, which means it's engaging with people who are not architects just as much as it's engaging with architects.

I think it's such a ridiculous notion that within our discipline we can only talk to architects. That's one aspect I just can't engage with. It's super banal and basically leads to a project of tastemaking rather than to an intellectual project. I think if it's going to be an intellectual project then it needs to expand beyond itself and constantly question its value system.

Isaac I think that the visual arts deal in emotion. That is often the language of expression as opposed to architecture, which we would discuss as more technical. How do we bring that subjecthood back into architectural conversations? I think a lot of the discussion is related to the techniques of emotion and feeling that comes with art.

KW This reminds me of something your colleague Amy Kulper brought up in the studio's final review. She referenced Richard Sennett's book *The Craftsman* and the notion of "repair" as the moment when we don't know where to go in a discipline and need to jump disciplines to find an answer. I've seen exactly

EMANUEL ADMASSU WITH KYLE WINSTON

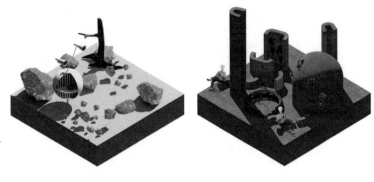

Caleb Dawoud Bey's photo series *Night Coming Tenderly, Black* was a huge reference for us. He takes these photographs that are super, super low exposure. It's very difficult to differentiate the different tones of gray and black, and it takes you a while to adjust to the image or to figure out what you're seeing. I think this is a really clear example of changing the expectations and conventions within the medium of photography and changing the way you have to read the image.

what she means in school recently, at least at the GSD. For example, beyond the visual arts, certain strains of critical theory have entered more and more into common discussion. To reconcile architecture's "complicit" role, we've turned to these ideas and techniques outside of architecture.

EA   It should have always been like this! You know what I mean? There's so much invention and radically different ways of looking at the world that are being presented by intellectuals outside of architecture. As spatial practitioners, if we don't engage with those ideas, then we're basically making ourselves irrelevant.

KW   What new tools have these other disciplines given us?

EA   There are certain commonalities that allow us to speak to one another. The potential of abstraction is something that can be shared across multiple disciplines. I think, for me, it's really about reading what these people have to say and trying to understand their spatial implications.

Sam I've been reflecting a lot recently on the inability of a plan and section to communicate projects or the mystification in which architecture exists. I think it holds back architects in general. There is a level of seriousness some images get that others don't; like a collage, people don't take it as seriously!

When I was in grad school, I took a seminar with Bernard Tschumi, and he had this notion at the time about architects always having to be at the edge of the discipline but always looking toward the center. This means that standing at the edge allows you to listen to what is happening in all the neighboring disciplines, but you're always looking toward the center. The only correction I would make to that is that I think you should be constantly looking toward the center and the periphery. I think there are times when you almost have to stop looking at the center.

Kyle What do you think now? Is property a good thing?

KW   Mm-hmm.

"AFTER PROPERTY" STUDIO IMAGERY

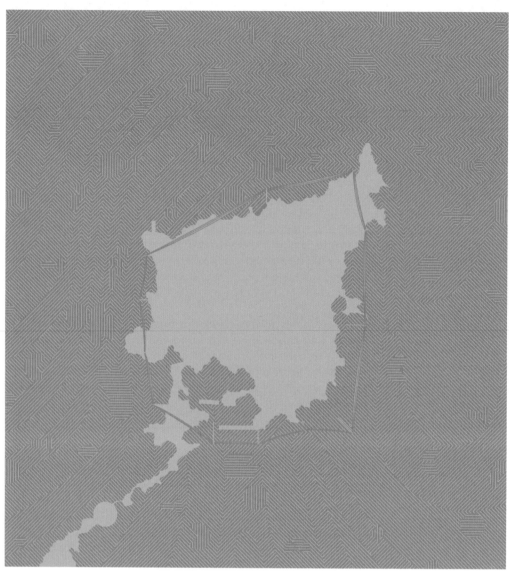

Bailey Property underrides the majority of our architectural work, but we never question it—its legitimacy, sovereignty, ownership, how that property came to be acquired, the legal definitions of a property, who has access to it and who doesn't, and then the architectural implications of what is being erected on that property, furthering certain ideas of possession.

"Palmares" project imagery exploring the cartographic representation of the Quilombo of Palmares, a settlement of escaped slaves in Brazil, and their present-day relation to the "heritage–industrial complex," such as UNESCO. The organization sets very specific expectations for sites, including who it belongs to, who it should be accessible to, who and where it came from, and how it should be managed. Created by Olivia Howard and Caleb Negash, fall 2020.

EMANUEL ADMASSU WITH KYLE WINSTON

Yifei We were heavily influenced by Linda Quiquivix's text, "Reparations Toward the End of the World," where she argues that the system has to be dismantled before the conversation of discrimination can even start.

Kathlyn I think we're all very hungry for this content. There's a lot of violence in architecture in its inaction and the image of neutrality architecture tries to put forth. This was a studio where neutrality was not an option—which was a breath of fresh air. It was difficult, but difficult and liberating because we were finally able to tackle issues that we know about but have not been formally educated on.

Yifei It was like nothing I had done before. After taking the studio, I realized that there was so much to learn. I had never really understood how architecture could become a tool in racism or borderization more generally.

"Home Sweet Not Home" project imagery speculating on a future where the apartment continues to "no longer be a place for living but [remains] analogous to depositing money in the bank." Created by Kyat Chin and Yifei Wu, fall 2020.

EA   Recently, because of my training and partnership and practice with Jen, I'm starting to feel more and more that we have to assume this attitude. We're calling it "art and architecture" mostly because we're doing a lot of research that can never really translate into buildings. That research has produced art objects, which is allowing us to expand the conversation. We're constantly looking inside and out. I'm not interested in just listening to the guys outside and looking toward the center.

Kathlyn Cindy and I latched onto Robin Coste Lewis's practice of redaction—it just blew our minds! The ways it allowed us to think about redacting ourselves or to understand opacity as a tool of resistance.

KW   I'm glad you brought up your work because I've been interested not only in your non-building work, such as the drawings for Two Markets, but also in your collaborations with artists, such as Ezra Wube, who I believe did illustrations for one of your exhibitions—

Bailey Because we do have tools to help solve these problems. I'm not saying they're going to be solved tomorrow, and I don't think anyone would.

EA   Yeah, he did the animation.

KW   Ah, okay. I'm wondering where you see the difference between what you do and what he does? The disciplinary line.

EA   That's a tough question. The way I think about it is, we're in conversation with each other, and the way I consume that conversation is going to be very different because of my training as an architect. The same goes for him as a fine artist. The most interesting part for us in all of these collaborations is

EMANUEL ADMASSU WITH KYLE WINSTON

finding a way to speak to people that don't necessarily speak our language.

That forces us not to settle with certain conventions and norms. I think what we bring to the table is always going to change depending on the context or the time we're living in.

KW   I see. It's not about the terms, it's about the frame of mind.

EA   And it's generative. I think when I have conversations with artists it makes me a better architect. Fundamentally. I mean, what kind of architecture comes out of it? I can never predetermine.

KW   I want to ask about that Tschumi anecdote, about being at the edge but looking toward the center. It's dependent in some way on there being a center at all, which seems more "disciplinary," more navel-gazing maybe, more autonomous, more … something. The edge needs the center in a way. So, how do you push the discipline and reject its norms while also relying on those norms to be there in order to be rejected?

EA   It's a really hard thing because we've been trained as architects to always contribute to the discipline, right? I don't really think that's my responsibility, personally. I think my responsibility is to be engaged with spatial issues and to speak to people that I find interesting and challenging. If that contributes to the discipline of architecture, great. If it doesn't or if it contributes to photography, to sculpture, even better.

Part of the contribution we have to make to the discipline is based on a need to destabilize it, a need to keep it from settling. I'm teaching a seminar right now called Disciplinarity, and we're primarily talking about these issues and how people have managed to become undisciplined. What type of intellectual project does that produce? You can look at this in almost every discipline. There are painters and sculptors who have managed to do it. I like thinking in these terms instead of through the tendencies in architecture academia that are really about policing or saying, "We have already determined what's valuable to architecture. If you can contribute to that, great. If not, then we don't need you around." That makes me react by saying, "Okay, you guys continue to have those conversations. I just won't be involved."

Cindy   One of the things Emanuel said that stuck with me is that we have to think about what architects actually contribute, what they actually do—which is make drawings. This gets into something that was addressed in the studio, which is about the creation of narratives and shedding more light on those that have been silenced. Storytelling through drawings is ultimately what the exercises with the sites and samples were trying to do.

Olivia   The studio was not so much about architects trying to do something else, but more trying to figure out how to use the tools that we do have to show something else.

KW   You've accepted and embraced that you're contributing somewhere, and it doesn't necessarily have to be under some predetermined umbrella. Are disciplinary boundaries important?

233

Caleb If what we're trying to do is this kind of subversive thing, should we really be trying to pull critical material from outside the discipline to bolster a discipline that we already have problems with? Is that fundamentally the goal? In a very direct sense it is. We're operating and doing this mode of inquiry under the auspices of a studio in a department of architecture at Harvard. There's that Reyner Banham essay, for example, where he talks about the "black box" of architecture and how it has this really specific 15th-century Italian disciplinary baggage. He basically says, "Well, maybe we should only call architecture that." That's the name we know. So maybe we do need a different term. It's true that not all buildings are architecture and not all architecture is about buildings.

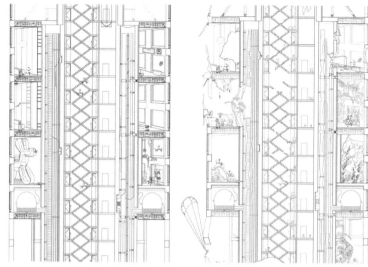

"Home Sweet Not Home" project sections highlighting the "physical and auditory presence" of service spaces in buildings like 432 Park Avenue, which manifest in door and wall types intended to promote discreet and often hidden human labor. Created by Kyat Chin and Yifei Wu, fall 2020.

EA   Yes, because you need something to react to or against. I think disciplinary positionality is kind of what allows you to be in practice. I'm glad the boundaries exist because I'm interested in perforating them as much as possible.

Sam Emanuel spoke with vulnerability. He wasn't authoritative; he communicated that we're all in this together.

KW   This is again where I get hung up. You want to perforate them, but you also want them to be there?

EA   Yes, because I think there is knowledge that is specific to disciplines. I can start painting tomorrow, but there's no way I would have all the knowledge of an art historian who might have studied the last 400 years of painting. I know I've dedicated a big chunk of my life to learning about architecture, and maybe that's what makes me an architect. I don't know. You can say that about photographers and graphic designers. You can enter into those realms, but people have spent a lot of time thinking about them. There's nuance there you can never pick up if you haven't dedicated the time.

Bailey I think we've had a better connection with the people in this studio than in almost any other.

KW   Do you think schools should be establishing clear frameworks for what the discipline is or distilling the discipline, in order to teach?

EA   No, no. I think the fundamental task is to frame some sort of collective intelligence within each course that is aware of the

EMANUEL ADMASSU WITH KYLE WINSTON

Kathlyn One of the things Emanuel always said was, "Excavate, excavate, excavate." I think that has become our new mantra. We need to keep looking. We need to keep finding counternarratives. We need to keep finding multiple perspectives that give us a whole understanding of the site and the problems we're trying to deal with as designers. At the GSD, it sometimes feels like an uphill battle because this hasn't been formally incorporated into our education.

Kyat We might not have necessarily solved anything, but it was good to excavate these hidden elements within our discourse that we don't normally question because we assume they're a given.

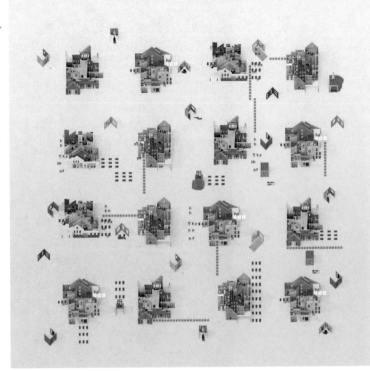

"Property, the Single-Family Home, and Trauma," or "Removing Bedrooms: Confronting Gendered Family Norms and Neoliberal Capitalism Toward a World After Property" project imagery. Created by Bailey Brown and Sam Sheffer, fall 2020.

Diandra At the end of the semester. We hadn't really designed or proposed a concrete solution. Maybe we presented this project as if it was going to lead somewhere, but in the end, it was all just up in the air, an idea of what could've been. I think that's completely valid. What we're proposing is a framework of thoughts and a way of juggling what already exists with how we as designers can project a new way of going about it.

history of the discipline and that can begin to speculate on where the discipline is heading. Giving answers on what the discipline is is not my job because I'm learning too. I mean, I want to be in a position where I am a student of the discipline, not professing what architecture is.

I'm also really interested in this more sneaky conversation that can happen when everyone is an architect but really wants to be a photographer or be a painter. You might make really terrible paintings but at least when you present them in the context of architecture they hopefully help us push some of the representational conversations forward.

KW Often after students engage with subjects like those in your studio and after their thesis (where they are presumably pushing the discipline's boundaries, asking new questions, etc.), they then gravitate back toward the discipline's center. They get a job at a corporate firm, join the AIA, and so on. A path like this is not creatively irredeemable, but it is no doubt

"AFTER PROPERTY" STUDIO IMAGERY

Isaac It was great to have all this in mind when we started our next, more "architectural" project. We started differently from how I think we would've otherwise. Do you think that's true or am I just …

Diandra No, I think it's true. We do now carry the sensibility and the questions we were forced to think about in the studio. I think it's healthy.

Isaac The studio had its contradictions, but I wouldn't call that a weakness, I would call it an honest take on what it is to be an architect grappling with these questions. There are going to be moments where you can't be so pure. You can't say, "I'm in the system" or "I'm out of the system." But you can strive for that. You can strive for an entirely new architecture. I think Emanuel really believes in that, and we believe in that too. He teaches architecture at institutions, and we study it at institutions —that in itself is a contradiction. That doesn't mean we can't have ambitions that go beyond where we are today.

Kyle Why did you take the studio?

Michele In Emanuel's first presentation, he spoke a lot about the meaning behind the word love and asked us, "What does it mean to put care into design?"

Bailey We created a lot of really ugly things along the way.

Sam I would agree.

Bailey Right? We created some really ugly objects, like some really ugly images. In trying to get at these issues of property, we were stuck in maps.

Sam I got stuck in portraiture of humans for a while.

"After Met" project imagery exploring the "Metropolitan Museum of Art's two conceptions of ownership: extraction and maintenance;" with the addition of "art racks," a "network allowing the collection to move in and out … so there is much less a permanent home." Created by Isaac Pollan and Diandra Rendradjaja, fall 2020.

more bureaucratically constrained. How do we reconcile this? How do we leverage these novel opportunities to maintain that fervor or that edge condition?

EA If I had the answer to that, I wouldn't be where I am! I used to try to think about these things generationally. When I was in grad school, a lot of people were feeling similarly to the way we are feeling right now. A lot of them were leaving the discipline and becoming curators. I think that sensibility has affected the way Jen and I think about our practice. In our case, I think we are also very much committed to making buildings. In every generation you're going to have some sort of bifurcation that is facilitated in part by what is happening in the world and in part by the shifting terrain of practice.

I think we are committed to doing things that excite us, and that's a very boring answer. But if I'm bored with redrawing the typical floor plan for a tower 100 times, then I need to

Bailey We sat in the backyard of Gund, in-person, and ate Triscuits, coming up with what we wanted from the project and what was operational moving forward. One of the things we talked a lot about was joy. In a space that's associated with trauma, how can it still have joy while being sensitive to those experiences? Trying to walk that line.

Sam We were saying, "We want to be realists, but we also want to be optimistic and joyful."

Bailey Optimism without utopianism. That was the stance we took. And in the development of the images, it pushed us further.

figure out something else to do, which might be a tapestry or it might be photography. There is an aspect of our discipline that is not nourishing at all, from an intellectual standpoint. So, we try our best to dodge that and find ways to stay engaged.

"AFTER PROPERTY" STUDIO IMAGERY

SUBJECTS AND OBJECTS

10   PAOLA STURLA
is a "architetto," "paesaggista,"
and full-time academic researching
artificial intelligence in design
practice. Born and raised in Italy,
Sturla holds a master's degree
in architecture from Politecnico
di Milano, as well as a Master in
Landscape Architecture from the
GSD. Currently, she teaches
landscape architecture at the GSD.

PHILIPS PAVILION
was commissioned by the electronics
manufacturer Philips and designed
by the office of Le Corbusier for Expo
58 in Brussels. While Le Corbusier
designed the Poème Électronique, a
technological spectacle for the
building's interior, the building's
form was envisionied by Iannis
Xenakis, who was then working for
the architect.

24   DAVID HARTT
is an artist and an associate professor at the University of Pennsylvania
School of Design in the Department
of Fine Arts. His work explores how
historic ideas and ideals persist
or transform over time. He lectured
at the GSD in spring 2019.

SHARON JOHNSTON
is an architect and the founder and
principal of the office Johnston
Marklee. She has designed numerous
projects, including the Menil
Drawing Institute and the UCLA
Graduate Arts Studios campus.
She and her partner Mark Lee, chair
of the Department of Architecture,
both hold the title of Professor in
Practice at the GSD.

STIRLING'S SKETCHES
OF SACKLER
are suite of drawings of James
Stirling's Arthur M. Sackler Building,
which was given to the Fogg Art
Museum by the architect in 1982. The
building is located on the campus
of Harvard University at 485 Broadway in Cambridge, Massachusetts.
It opened in October 1985.

44   JOHN R. STILGOE
is the Robert and Lois Orchard
Professor in the History of
Landscape, jointly appointed in the
Harvard Faculties of Arts and
Science and the GSD. He has
taught at Harvard since finishing
his PhD in 1976.

SEVER HALL GRAFFITO
is a photograph by John R. Stilgoe
that shows the graffito "Kent State
4 Dead" which was scrawled onto
the brickwork of Harvard's Sever
Hall in response to the shootings of
students by the Ohio National Guard
at Kent State University in 1970.
Although repeatedly cleaned by the
university, the words are still
visible in particular light at certain
times of the year.

239

54

RASHID BIN SHABIB
is an urbanist and co-creator of
Brownbook magazine with his
twin brother Ahmed bin Shabib.
Based in Dubai, he has exhibited
and lectured widely and holds
a master's degree in sustainable
urbanism from the University
of Oxford.

GARETH DOHERTY
is a landscape architect, theorist,
and educator who has lectured and
taught extensively. Doherty is an
associate professor of landscape
architecture and the director of
the Master in Landscape Architecture program at the GSD.

**TANGE'S DRAWINGS
OF ST. MARY'S**
are competition entry drawings for
the building and are part of the
Kenzō Tange Archive in the Special
Collections of Loeb Library at the
GSD. Given to the school in 2011
by Takako Tange, the archive is
composed of architectural drawings,
architectural models, clippings,
manuscript notebooks, and print
publications.

74

MALKIT SHOSHAN
is the founding director of the
Amsterdam and New York-based
architectural think tank FAST:
Foundation for Achieving Seamless
Territory. She has been a lecturer
in architecture at the GSD since
fall of 2016.

**MISSIONARY, UN, AND
TUAREG TENTS**
are a set of photographs and models,
all by Shoshan, that establish a
visual lexicon of tents in Africa. They
display visible differences between
the institutional structures
made for current UN peacekeeping
efforts and the historical tents
of nomadic peoples and missionary
endeavors.

86

IRMA BOOM
is an Amsterdam-based graphic
designer with a specialty in
bookmaking. In the fall of 2018,
she gave a public lecture at
the GSD in which she shared
books from the entirety of her
career.

THE VERGILIUS VATICANUS
is a manuscript, also known as the
Vatican Virgil, which was made
in Rome around 400 CE and now
resides in the Vatican Library. It
is the oldest and one of only three
illustrated manuscripts of classical
literature and contains fragments
of Virgil's *Aeneid* and *Georgics*.

100

KATHRYN YUSOFF
is professor of inhuman geography
at Queen Mary University of London
whose research examines how
nonorganic dimensions of life have
consequences for how we understand issues related to fossil fuels
and the politics of human–earth
relations. She delivered a lecture at
the GSD in 2020 titled, "Geo-Logics:
Natural Resources as Necropolitics."

IMAGES NOT AVAILABLE
is a screenshot of the online database of Harvard's Peabody Museum
of Archaeology and Ethnology.
The collection shown, a majority of
which has yet to be digitized,
contains photographs from Louis
Agassiz's 19th-century expeditions
to South America and Africa to
document ethnographic subjects.

110   **JORGE SILVETTI**
is the Nelson Robinson, Jr. professor of architecture and a former
chair of the GSD's Department
of Architecture. He has taught
at the GSD for over four decades,
while concurrently running the
international practice Machado
Silvetti.

LABYRINTH OF AFFINITIES
is a set of images and references
assembled by the authors especially for this conversation. The
labyrinth contextualizes the
experiences and projects of Jorge
Silvetti alongside a discussion
of larger disciplinary issues and
cultural processes.

126   **SARA HENDREN**
is an artist, design researcher,
and writer who teaches design for
disability at Olin College of
Engineering. She holds an MDes in
Art, Design, and the Public Domain
(with distinction) from the GSD.

**NEARLY ME BREAST
PROSTHETIC**
is an image of Ruth Handler display-
ingthe two-time breast cancer
survivor as the inventor of Nearly
Me mastectomy products, which
have been on the market since 1976.
Handler is the creator of the
original Barbie doll and is a former
CEO of the Mattel Corporation.

136   **LYNDON NERI**
is a founding partner of Neri&Hu
Design and Research Office,
an interdisciplinary practice based
in Shanghai. Alongside Rossana
Hu, he recently taught a studio as
a John C. Portman design critic
at the GSD.

**SKETCHES FOR A
SCARPA SHOW**
are drawings by Lyndon Neri for the
Carlo Scarpa exhibition *Traversing
Thresholds* that opened in
November 2021 at the MAXXI in
Rome. Part of a series, the
exhibition is a collaborative project
where designers are invited
to interpret items in the museum's
archive and work with curators to
design the installation.

152   **DAVID FOSTER**
is an ecologist, author, and director
of the Harvard Forest. He teaches
forest ecology and has studied
the forests of Labrador, Sweden,
Norway, Puerto Rico, the Yucatan,
and Patagonia in addition to his
primary research on the landscape
dynamics of New England.

ZACHARY MOLLICA
is an architect and warden of the
Architectural Association's Hooke
Park campus, a forest and architectural research site focused on
1:1 fabrication with advanced
technologies and woods harvested
on site.

**HEMLOCK RINGS AND
TREE FORKS**
are a cross section of a large
Hemlock and index of tree forks that
establish two different ways of
cataloging the growth patterns and
diversity of forms found in the
arboreal world. Viewed side-by-side
the differing strategies offer a way
to juxtapose the values of analog
and digital means for visualizing and
understanding forests.

241

176

SUMAYYA VALLY
is the founder and principal of Counterspace, an architecture studio based in Johannesburg, South Africa. The office designed the 2021 Serpentine Pavilion. Vally was part of the jury for the GSD's 2021 Wheelwright Prize.

ISLAMIC HERITAGE PROJECT
is a Harvard University effort to catalog, conserve, and digitize hundreds of Islamic manuscripts, maps, and published texts from the university's renowned library and museum collections. Visualizing materials from the 10th to 20th centuries, the project encompasses myriad subjects from across the Islamic world.

194

TERRY TEMPEST WILLIAMS
is a Utah-based writer, educator, and environmental activist. She is currently the writer-in-residence at Harvard Divinity School, where she writes about and leads seminars on the spiritual implications of climate change.

AARON SISKIND'S *UTAH* SERIES
is a set of photographs owned by the Harvard Art Museums/Fogg Museum completed by the artist in the 1970s in Utah. The abstraction of natural forms at close proximity enables a new scrutiny through a dissociative perspective of things otherwise known.

210

JANE MAH HUTTON
is a landscape architect and assistant professor at the University of Waterloo whose research examines the movement of materials and the invisible landscapes of production. Hutton was previously an assistant professor at the GSD, where she helped establish the Materials Collection.

NEW ENGLAND ERRATICS
feature images a part of the Gardner Photography Collection of the Cabot Science Library at Harvard University and were featured in the GSD's 2010 exhibition *Erratics: A Genealogy of Rock Landscape*. Erratics are rocks that have moved by geological forces, especially during the last Ice Age.

218

EMANUEL ADMASSU
is an assistant professor at the Columbia University Graduate School of Architecture, Planning and Preservation. With Jen Wood, he is a founding partner of AD–WO, an art and architecture practice based in New York City. Admassu taught the studio "After Property" at the GSD in the fall of 2020.

"AFTER PROPERTY" STUDIO IMAGERY
are images created for the studio taught virtually by Emanuel Admassu at the GSD in the fall of 2020. Working in pairs, students developed "sites" and "samples," emblematic of present regimes and imagery, proposing an architecture disentangled from the concept of property.

242

EDITORS, CONTRIBUTORS, DESIGNERS

EDITORS

NICOLÁS DELGADO ÁLCEGA is a 2020 graduate of the GSD Master in Architecture II program and holds an undergraduate degree from the University of Miami, where he also studied architecture. He is from Caracas, Venezuela.

VLADIMIR GINTOFF is a 2021 graduate of the GSD Master in Architecture I and Master in Urban Planning programs and holds an undergradate degree from Tisch School of the Arts at New York University, where he studied photography and art history. He lives in Brooklyn, New York.

KIMBERLEY HUGGINS is a 2020 graduate of the GSD Master in Landscape Architecture program and holds an undergraduate degree from the University of Western Ontario, where she studied biomedical and environmental science. She is from Toronto, Canada.

KYLE WINSTON is a fourth-year GSD Master in Architecture I student with an undergraduate degree in architecture from the College of Design, Architecture, Art, and Planning at the University of Cincinnati. He is from Delaware, Ohio.

CONTRIBUTORS

EMMA LEWIS is a 2021 graduate of the GSD Master in Design Studies program in Critical Conservation and holds an undergraduate degree in sociology from Kenyon College. She is from Arlington, Massachusetts.

ELISA NGAN is a GSD Master in Design Engineering student and holds an undergraduate degree from the University of California, Berkeley, where she studied architecture. She is from San Francisco, California.

MAXWELL SMITH-HOLMES is a 2021 graduate of the GSD Master in Landscape Architecture program and holds an undergraduate degree from Reed College, where he studied art history. He is from Seattle, Washington.

DESIGNERS

NORMAL is a graphic design practice based in Chicago, Illinois. Normal believes thoughtful design and collaboration strengthen our collective knowledge and define new ways of seeing, communicating, and experiencing the world. Normal is Renata Graw, Lucas Reif, and Noël Morical.

ARYN BEITZ is a graphic designer and writer based in Pittsburgh, Pennsylvania. She currently works as the director of design and publishing at the Carnegie Museum of Art. Previously, she worked as a designer at the Shed in New York and at the Walker Art Center in Minneapolis, Minnesota. She holds an MFA in Communications Design from Pratt Institute.

IMAGE CREDITS

DISCLAIMER

The editors of *Pairs* are grateful for all permissions to reproduce copyrighted material in this issue. Every effort has been made to trace the ownership of copyrighted material and to secure proper credits and permissions from the appropriate copyright holders. In the event of any omission or oversight, please contact the editorial team and all necessary corrections will be made in future printings.

PAOLA STURLA

12-15: Courtesy of Fondation Le Corbusier.
18-21: Scans provided by Harvard Widener Library. Courtesy of Fondation Le Corbusier.

DAVID HARTT & SHARON JOHNSTON

26-28, 32-33, 36-37, 40-41: Courtesy of Harvard Art Museums/ Fogg Museum, Gift of James Stirling. © James Stirling, Photo © President and Fellows of Harvard College.

JOHN R. STILGOE

46: Courtesy of John R. Stilgoe
50: Courtesy of the Frances Loeb Library, Harvard Graduate School of Design (4045).

RASHID BIN SHABIB & GARETH DOHERTY

57-59, 62-65, 70-71: Courtesy of Tange, Kenzō (1913-2005). The Kenzo Tange Archive, Gift of Takako Tange, 2011. St. Mary's Cathedral (Tokyo), Folder A052. Courtesy of the Frances Loeb Library, Harvard University Graduate School of Design.

MALKIT SHOSHAN

76-78, 80, 82: Courtesy of Foundation for Achieving Seamless Territory (FAST)/Malkit Shoshan.

IRMA BOOM

91-92, 95: By permission of Biblioteca Apostolica Vaticana, with all rights reserved.

KATHRYN YUSOFF

102: Courtesy of Kathryn Yusoff
104-105: Courtesy of the Peabody Museum of Archaeology and Ethnology, Harvard University, 2004.24.7646.

JORGE SILVETTI

123-124: Collage courtesy of its authors (Jorge Silvetti and Nicolás Delgado Álcega). Authors have made every attempt to use image thumbnails according to fair use, showing only as much as necessary for referential/ transformative purposes.

SARA HENDREN

128: Courtesy of Schlesinger Library, Harvard Radcliffe Institute.

LYNDON NERI

139, 141, 143, 145, 147, 149: Courtesy of Neri&Hu Design and Research Office.

ZACHARY MOLLICA & DAVID FOSTER

156-158: Courtesy of Mariela Reyes.
159: Courtesy of Zachary Mollica.
164-165: Courtesy of Harvard Forest Archives.
166, 168-171: Courtesy of Zachary Mollica.
172-173: Courtesy of David Foster.

SUMAYYA VALLY

178, 181: Courtesy of Islamic Heritage Project, MS Arab 309. Houghton Library, Harvard University.

182, 185, 186–187: Courtesy of Islamic Heritage Project, MS Arab 374. Houghton Library, Harvard University.

188–189: Courtesy of Islamic Heritage Project, MS Persian 34. Houghton Library, Harvard University.

190, 193: Courtesy of Islamic Heritage Project, MS Arab 18. Houghton Library, Harvard University.

TERRY TEMPEST WILLIAMS

197, 199, 202–203, 205, 207: Image scans provided by the Harvard Art Museums. Harvard Art Museums/Fogg Museum, Gift of Carl Chiarenza and Heidi Katz in memory of Charles and Mary Chiarenza. Copyright Estate of Aaron Siskind.

JANE MAH HUTTON

212: Courtesy of the Cabot Science Library, Harvard University.

214: Jotham A. French. Gardner. Courtesy of the Cabot Science Library, Harvard University.

EMANUEL ADMASSU

220: Courtesy of Harvard GSD students Olivia Howard and Caleb Negash.

222–224: Courtesy of Harvard GSD students Kathlyn Kao and Cindy Yiin.

226: Courtesy of Harvard GSD students Isaac Pollan and Diandra Rendradjaja.

228–229: Courtesy of Harvard GSD students Michele Chen and Keira Li.

230–231: Courtesy of Harvard GSD students Olivia Howard and Caleb Negash.

232, 234: Courtesy of Harvard GSD students Kyat Chin and Yifei Wu.

235: Courtesy of Harvard GSD students Bailey Brown and Sam Sheffer.

236: Courtesy of Harvard GSD students Isaac Pollan and Diandra Rendradjaja.

IMAGE CREDITS